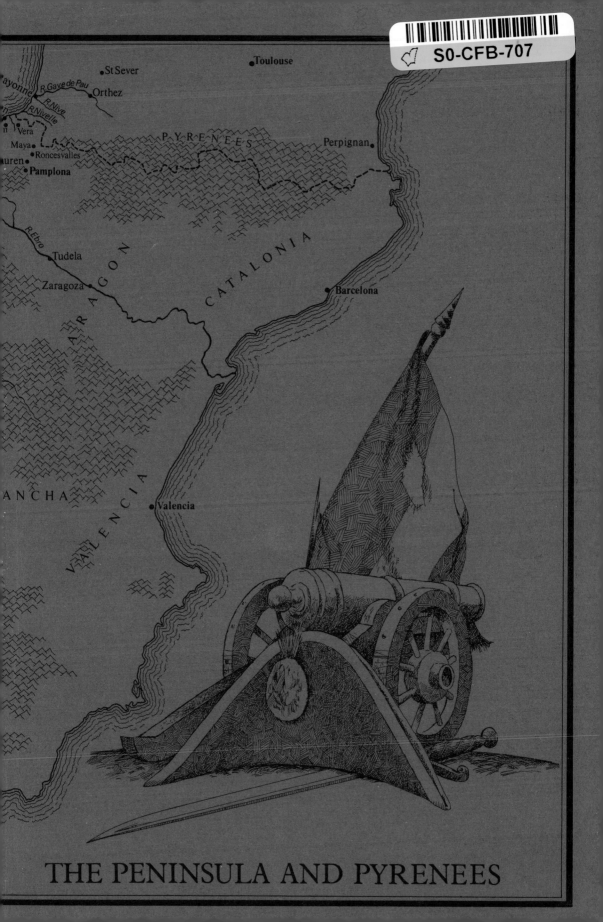

St Sever

Toulouse

Bayonne

R.Gave de Pau

Orthez

R.Nive

R.Nivelle

Vera

P Y R E N E E S

Perpignan

Maya

Roncesvalles

uren

Pamplona

R.Ebro

C A T A L O N I A

A R A G O N

Tudela

Zaragoza

Barcelona

V A L E N C I A

ANCHA

Valencia

# THE PENINSULA AND PYRENEES

The
Peninsular
War

# The British
## at War

General Editor:
Ludovic Kennedy

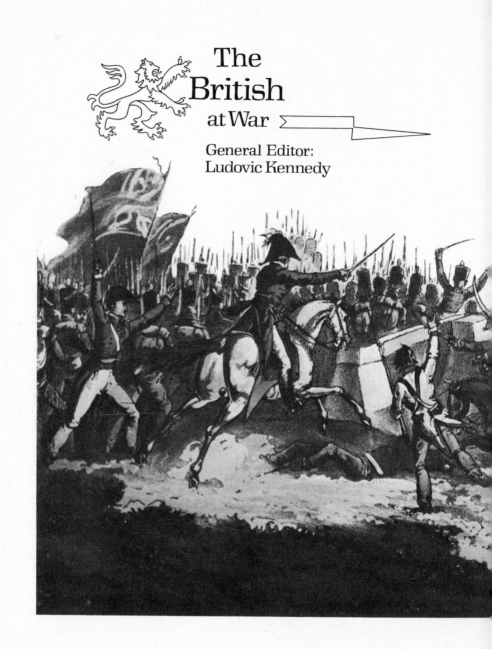

Roger Parkinson

# The
# Peninsular
## War

Hart-Davis MacGibbon London

Granada Publishing Limited
First published 1973 by Hart-Davis, MacGibbon Ltd
Park Street, St Albans, Hertfordshire and
3 Upper James Street, London W1R 4BP

ISBN 0 246 64096 0

Filmset by Keyspools Limited, Golborne, Lancs
Printed in Great Britain by C. Tinling & Co Ltd,
Prescot & London

# Contents

# Acknowledgements

The photographs and illustrations in this book are reproduced by kind permission of the following. Those on pages 106, 161 and 175, the Duke of Wellington, M.V.O., O.B.E., M.C.; pages 24, 30, 31, 67, 86, 130–31, 140, 158, 176, 192, 195, 199 and 204, National Army Museum; pages 10, 20, 21, 22–3, 44–5, 51, 82, 107, 120, 125, 129, 165, 173, 182, 189 and 201, British Museum; pages 13, 14, 15, 16, 34–5, 73, 85, 88, 97, 118, 126–7, 133, 142, 144, 151, 162, 164, 166, 170, 178, 181, 186 and 190, Radio Times Hulton Picture Library; pages 8, 19, 53, 76, 79, 80 and 147, National Portrait Gallery; pages 28, 29, 31, 54, 148, 163, 177, 188 and 203, Wellington Museum; page 105, National Gallery; pages 33, 57, 90, 157 and 176 (top), Mansell Collection; pages 26–7 and 123, Bulloz, Paris; page 25, Scala, Milan; page 72, Prado, Madrid; page 111, Portuguese Tourist Office; page 124, Barnaby's Picture Library; page 68, Yale University Art Gallery; page 139, Royal Green-jackets Regimental Museum; pages 58 and 62–3, S. J. Dickinson Esq.; the picture on page 71 is from a private collection. Illustration Research Service supplied the pictures. The maps were drawn by Brian and Constance Dear.

# Introduction

Today's generation thinks of 'guerilla warfare'—whether in south-east Asia, the Congo, Cuba or Ulster—as a mainly modern phenomenon. In fact, although guerilla warfare started when man first ambushed his neighbour, it was during the famous Peninsular campaign of Arthur Wellesley, future Duke of Wellington, that the name 'guerilla', meaning 'little war', was coined. This book shows the relationship between regular forces and guerilla fighters, from which lessons can be learned today.

In the whole context of Napoleon's military career, the Peninsular War was of critical importance. Of all his setbacks, including even the disastrous campaign of 1812, he regarded his 'Spanish ulcer' as the most crippling.

Roger Parkinson has made skilful use of the wealth of letters, diaries and eye-witness accounts of the war left by officers and men. They complement the many contemporary prints and paintings, and show the glories and disappointments, excesses and discomforts of what professionals on both sides regarded as an unusually tough campaign.

Ludovic Kennedy

# Chapter 1

# Spanish Ulcer

Horses clattered over the Lisbon cobbles to pull a careering coach down towards the bustling harbour. Inside the ornate carriage swayed Queen Marie, insane for the last twenty years, and her son John, Prince Regent. Before them lay the broad Tagus river and British warships ready to take the royal family to Brazil. Behind them, a few miles from Portugal's capital, filed a dusty column of 1,500 tattered and tired French troops commanded by the Burgundy woodsman's son, Andoche Junot. His task on this 30 November 1807, was to impose his Emperor Napoleon's will upon the impertinent Portuguese who had refused to enforce the blockade against Britain. The old, mad Queen leant forward and shouted at her sweating coachman. 'Slow down!' she shrilled. 'Or the people will think we're fleeing.' Within minutes the Queen and her ineffectual son had safely fled; within hours her abandoned Lisbon citizens heard the first faint tappings on the approaching French drums. Elegant, perfumed Lisbon ladies crowded the balconies to watch the filthy and exhausted invasion troops arrive, while Queen Marie rested in the competent hands of Graham Moore, captain of the 3-decker, 74-gun HMS *Marlborough*. Captain Moore's brother was to die in agony at Corunna fourteen months later. The occupation of Portugal, and the flight of the royal family, marked a major stepping-stone to the fascinating and unique Peninsular War – condemned by Napoleon as his 'Spanish ulcer'.

From the high Pyrenees to the burnt Sierra Morena, the Peninsular War was a conflict of contrasts. Wellington's 'family' of gaily uniformed officers, with their dashing, debonair attitude to battle, their aristocratic ease, their youthful good looks, fought alongside the guerrillas and partisans under El Empecinado or Merino the Priest – ragged, barbaric and equally effective. The war saw a further contrast between both infinite cruelty and remarkable courtesy. Troops plundered and pillaged, and the British were hardly better than the rest: the successful storming of Ciudad Rodrigo and Badajoz, in January and April 1812, resulted in an orgy of destruction by Wellington's drunken men, when women were raped, children spitted upon bloody bayonets, babies battered to death. The only excuse offered was that 'the French were worse'. Indeed they were, especially against the guerrillas or those suspected of helping these rebels – men or women. Torture by

*Opposite* Napoleon Bonaparte, sleek, confident, at the peak of his power when the Peninsular War opened in 1807; he was 38, one year younger than Wellington. *From the painting by T. Heaphie*

9

Andoche Junot, aged 35 when Napoleon gave him the Portuguese command, came to the Peninsula covered in glory from his campaigning in Italy and Egypt.

disembowelling or burning became widespread, practised on both sexes; these atrocities were only matched by those perpetrated upon the French by the guerrillas themselves. Reprisal fed upon repulsive reprisal. And yet a dash of gentleness mingled with this horror. A minimum of hatred existed between British and French troops, especially during winter seasons when the tempo of war slowed.

Forage parties exchanged compliments and items of uniform, wounded prisoners usually received sympathetic care, and many are the tales of friendly contact outside the actual brutal business of fighting. Wellington frowned upon killing for the mere sake of slaughter. 'The killing of a poor fellow of a vedette (scout) . . . could not influence the battle and I always . . . sent to tell them to get out of the way.' On at least one occasion sentry duties were shared: a British soldier paced up and down for a while, French musket slung on one shoulder, his own weapon on the other, before being relieved by his enemy colleague. Also most of the British soldiers preferred their French enemy to their Spanish hosts.

The war was both modern and old-fashioned; it had a modern, total aspect in that all strata of population were dragged into the maelstrom, and yet the war retained some of the semi-civilised rules of previous times, which specified campaigning seasons and correct conduct towards the opposing forces. This was the conflict which began with Napoleon at the peak of his incredible power and ended with his attempted suicide. The war started with the young Sir Arthur Wellesley as the eighth in the official line of command in the Peninsula, and saw his rise to the title of Duke of Wellington and to the position of Britain's greatest general. Hostilities opened with the British army discredited, and even during the course of the war Wellington described his men as 'scum', but by the close Spain had been swept clean and the now famous veterans were stabbing into southern France. And the conflict led to the emergence of a new form of war on a larger scale than ever before: the deadly weapon provided by a guerrilla force operating in conjunction with a regular army.

Campaigns stimulated all the senses. The sight of the magnificent mountains and the endless, shimmering plains; the plumes and pennants of the armies; the acres of dead. The sound of the enemy drums – four beats, a roll, two beats; the shrieking ungreased wheels of the Portuguese oxen-carts; the screams of the wounded. The feel of the ice in the high passes, which froze faces and stuck top lip to lower, and the heat in the wastes, which crazed men through thirst and made muskets too hot to hold. The smell of orange blossom, or the rotting victims of last week's battle rooted from shallow graves by wolves.

This was the Peninsular War. A war of extremes, of innovation, horror, excitement and drudgery. And a war which should never have begun at all.

Never would Napoleon Bonaparte bask in such glory as on the wet day of 25 June 1807. The Emperor had inflicted crushing defeats upon the outdated Prussian armies at Jena and Auerstadt the previous October, and on 14 June had routed the Russians at Friedland. Now, on the afternoon of the 25th, he was rowed out to a log raft in the middle of the frontier river Niemen to meet the Russian Emperor Alexander. The Prussian Emperor, Friedrich Wilhelm, was obliged to wait in the pouring rain on the sodden river bank. Napoleon, having conquered the Russian armies, now sought the diplomatic defeat of the thirty-year-old Alexander through his considerable charm. The campaign proved pleasant: Alexander was blue-eyed, pretty, with blond curls, and Napoleon commented: 'Were he a woman, I think I should fall passionately in love with him.' After hours of sweet conversation on the gently swaying raft, Alexander returned the compliment. 'Why didn't I meet him before?' he complained with delight. The Treaty of Tilsit resulted: Prussia lost all her territory between the Elbe and Rhine rivers; Russia on the other hand was only asked to agree to an alliance with France – against Britain. Napoleon's prime aim was to isolate Britain, now the only major power in effective opposition to him. The Royal Navy blockaded the European coast, but Napoleon had imposed a counter-blockade through his Continental System in November 1806. After Tilsit, neutral Portugal remained the only access route for British trade to the Continent, save by smuggling.

So Napoleon's gaze was now directed to the far side of Europe – to the Peninsula. Spain was officially ruled by Charles IV, but this monarch was dominated by his wife, Maria Luisa, who was herself under the influence of her lover, Manuel Godoy. Napoleon benefited from this twisted triangle: Godoy had persuaded Charles to conclude the Treaty of Basle with the French in 1795 and Spain had become an ally of France. Portugal therefore constituted the single thorn in the Empire's sensitive nether regions, and in the winter of 1807 Napoleon was determined to pluck it out. To do this, Spanish permission was obtained for Junot's army to hurry through for the invasion of Portugal in November. Lisbon was taken. On 17 December the Milan Decree reaffirmed the Continental System against Britain; British trade was banned from all Europe. But now smuggling became more widespread – especially through the Spanish ports. Napoleon decided upon determined action, and tangled intrigue at the Spanish court seemed to give him the desired opening.

The corrupt and inefficient Spanish monarchy was split into

factions headed by Charles IV, by the Crown Prince Ferdinand, and by Godoy. Riots and plots were rife. In October 1807, Charles and his son Ferdinand separately sought French help, much to Napoleon's delight. Each faction accused the other of seeking to overthrow rivals and obtain supreme power: Charles accused Ferdinand of intended assassination and treason, and had him arrested. Napoleon began to move troops into Spain, on the pretexts of reinforcing Junot in Portugal and of guarding Spanish coasts, and at the same time he made tempting offers both to Godoy – described by him privately as 'a prize bull' – and to Ferdinand. In mid-March 1808, Madrid citizens revolted against their rulers; Napoleon's brother-in-law Murat hastened towards the capital to take advantage of the upheaval. Charles was obliged to abdicate in favour of Ferdinand. Napoleon called the faction leaders to Bayonne: Ferdinand was accused by Godoy and by his parents of being a bastard, and the dynasty was dismissed. Napoleon named his elder brother, Joseph, as King of Spain, and the new ruler entered his kingdom on 9 June.

But already rebellion had flared. Guerrilla warfare swept the countryside; French troops were forced back into their garrisons

Madrid riots, 1808, as the Spanish people rise against the French invaders – opposition which Napoleon vastly underestimated.

13

The Spanish Insurrec-
tion of 2 May 1808,
painted by Goya. This
brutal repression by the
French merely strength-
ened support for the
partisans.

and Murat fell back to the Ebro. Junot was isolated in Portugal.
British money and equipment began to seep into the country.
More substantial help was immediately sought by both Spain
and Portugal, and in the first week of June two members of the
Spanish Government arrived in England on board a borrowed
pirate vessel, to receive an enthusiastic welcome from Foreign
Minister George Canning. Britain proclaimed peace with Spain
on 4 July; an expedition to Portugal was prepared.

Such an operation was extremely attractive to the British
Government, which had a preference for this kind of expedition.
But so far similar schemes had met with unfortunate results –
including the ill-fated attempt in the Low Countries in 1799 and
the abortive plan to help Sweden in early 1808 – and the British
army had still to recover from the humiliation suffered at the hands
of the American rebels, who had won their independence in 1783.
Yet hopes now ran high, and with good reason. Napoleon had made
a disastrous mistake in believing he could tack Spain meekly to his
empire. Spain, unlike Germany or Italy, was a single nation; her

14

people had long loyalties and pride in the past. The Pyrenees had been a symbol of Spanish independence from the rest of Europe, and the people were determined this barrier should remain. Moreover, while Britain and Portugal had been allies since the Middle Ages, relations with Spain were the reverse. Only a century before, British troops had invaded the country; Napoleon should have fed this latent ill-feeling, rather than allowing it to be glossed over. And Napoleon suffered intense disadvantages once Spanish opposition arose: his forces could be linked to France only by tenuous communications, easily severed by guerrillas; the country-side itself offered excellent opportunities for this guerrilla warfare; Britain could make full use of her prime weapon – sea power. Spanish patriots and British commanding officers could ensure fighting was dispersed throughout the Peninsula; Napoleon might be able to win battles, but winning the war would be infinitely more difficult. His usual strategy, of concentrating his forces upon the crucial point in order to gain a decisive victory, was now far less effective. And the more the French had to struggle in the Peninsula morass, the more those subjugated people elsewhere became stimulated into revolt. Napoleon should have left Spain well alone; the advantages to be gained in adding that country to his Empire were far outweighed by the difficulties involved. Spain, the last card to be added to his Empire castle, was to help send the whole pack tumbling down. ⇒

One bull too many: the Spanish beast tosses Napoleon and tramples Joseph, watched by the Pope and the European rulers.

The SPANISH BULL FIGHT or the CORSICAN MATADOR in Danger.

# Chapter 2

# Vimiero
# Victory

Two men now hoped and expected to command the British army in the Peninsula. Sir John Moore and Sir Arthur Wellesley shared many similarities: both were young – Moore, in 1808, was forty-seven and Wellesley only thirty-nine; both were handsome, Moore with his boyish grin and curly fair hair, Wellesley with his dark good looks; they each tended to be withdrawn, even diffident, hated ostentatious dress or behaviour; inspired quiet confidence among their officers and worship from their troops. Both were extremely intelligent, quick-acting in battle, brilliant tacticians. They were Britain's most promising young lieutenant-generals – Sir Arthur Wellesley having only been given this rank on 25 April for his handling of the British forces during the expedition to Denmark.

In early July 1808, Wellesley was in Cork, commander of 9,000 men being made ready to invade Spanish America; Moore was sailing back to Britain after a bizarre expedition to Sweden – he had been sent with an expeditionary force empowered to assist the Swedish king in the defence of his country; instead Gustavus IV had failed to persuade Moore to undertake a hopeless offensive against Russia, and had put the British general under arrest. Moore had escaped disguised as a peasant, and was now expected to land at Yarmouth on the 15th. Meanwhile, Wellesley received fresh instructions. The destination of his force had been switched from Spanish America to the Peninsula: Spain was no longer an enemy but an ally in need of help. Wellesley's 9,000 men were to be reinforced on arrival by 5,000 troops under General Sir Brent Spencer, which were already in the area. Spencer was to be his second-in-command. Wellesley's hopes for the Peninsula command therefore seemed fulfilled, and he put to sea on 12 July, transferring to the fast cruiser *Crocodile* on the 13th – the same day that his army sailed. During a silent moment a few days before, he had been asked his thoughts and had replied: 'Of the French, I have never seen them; they have beaten all Europe. I think I shall beat them, but I can't help thinking about them.' Wellesley was both confident and content. But on 16 June Sir John Moore learnt that neither he nor Wellesley would enjoy the privilege of the Peninsula command. He was told to proceed to Portugal, where his troops would join those already sailing under Wellesley, but the total army, numbering about 30,000, would be led by Sir Hew Dalrymple – who had not fought on a battlefield for over fourteen years. Under Sir Hew would be Sir Harry Burrard, aged seventy-three. Sir John Moore, to be only third in the line, took the arrange-

*Opposite* A Scottish soldier at Vimiero finds time in the heat of close-range combat to plead for the life of an enemy cavalryman.

17

ment as a personal insult, as indeed it was: King George III had expressed the opinion that Moore had been involved in a political plot to get his troops away from Sweden, so that he could command them in Spain. Moore nevertheless sailed from Portsmouth on a drizzling Sunday, 31 July 1808. He would never again see the coast of Britain.

Moore's voyage would take sixteen days. Meanwhile, events had quickened in the Peninsula. On 23 July came the first surrender of a Napoleonic army, after General Pierre Dupont, having manoeuvred his 30,000 men into an impossible position near Baylen, and after hesitating too long before withdrawing, had found himself surrounded by Spanish forces under General Castaños. Both commanders behaved with considerable incompetence, but the Spaniard managed to keep the advantage and Dupont capitulated. Over 18,000 French troops were obliged to lay down their arms: many of these men were then immediately massacred. The victory had a number of consequences: the battle was generally believed to have been won by armed peasants, and hence roused tremendous enthusiasm throughout Spain; in reality the peasants had played a secondary role to the regular Spanish forces – many of these being Swiss mercenaries – and this in turn gave the Spanish army unwarranted confidence. In Portugal, Junot's isolation was further emphasised; and next day Sir Arthur Wellesley reached Oporto. He left again the following morning, 25 July, aiming further south at Mondego Bay, where landings would be made for the advance on Lisbon. Mondego was reached on the 30th. The same day one of the French generals in Portugal, Loison, ensured Wellesley even greater support from the Portuguese by his massacre of men, women and babies at Evora; anti-French feeling reached fever heat, and French mistakes, both military and political, seemed to justify Wellesley's increasing confidence. But, also at Mondego, Sir Arthur discovered the unwieldy system of command in the Peninsula which had been decreed by ministers in London. The official seniority list in the Peninsula, issued on 20 July, had placed Wellesley at the bottom in eighth position, after Sir Hew Dalrymple, Sir Harry Burrard, Sir John Moore, Sir John Hope, Sir Kenneth Mackenzie, General Fraser and Lord Paget. Sir Arthur Wellesley had only one consolation: Sir Hew and Sir Harry were still *en route* with the other four lieutenant-generals, and Sir John Moore was sailing independently with his force. Hence Wellesley was told by Castlereagh, Secretary of War, that until the arrival of these other officers he was to continue his preparations against Lisbon on his own initiative; a

A youthful Sir Arthur Wellesley, depicted by an unknown artist just before his departure for Portugal.

letter to the Duke of Richmond revealed Wellesley's appreciation of this temporary escape clause: 'I hope that I shall have beat Junot before any of them arrive, then they will do as they please with me.' On 1 August a myriad of small craft left the warships heaving on the swell and began to cut through the pounding surf to land British troops on Portuguese soil.

These were the men upon whom Britain relied to repolish her tarnished military image. Many were young raw recruits, some of them barely sixteen years of age, who had succumbed to appealing posters: 'WANTED – Brisk Lads, light and straight, and by no 19

Sir Hew Dalrymple, Commander-in-Chief in Portugal, aged almost 60 and who had only once before seen active service in the disastrous 1793 Flanders campaign.

means gummy: not under 5 feet 5½ inches, or over 5 feet 9 inches in height. Liberal bounty; good uniforms; generous pay! Step lively, lads, and come in while there is time!...' But few people at home – except young boys – envied the life of a soldier; the infantryman was frequently looked upon with justification as a drunkard and ne'er-do-well, and was considered to be on a level with the common criminal – indeed many of them were, having found themselves in the ranks through the ability of recruiting officers to pay off fines and debts. Foot-soldiers in the Peninsula would soon find they had a new nickname: 'caracho' – a corruption of 'caranga', meaning louse. Those in the cavalry enjoyed greater prestige, and this attitude of greater glory was lavishly used to

persuade country boys to enlist as troopers: huge placards were plastered in London and the Home Counties, for example, proclaiming the honour of joining 'Elliott's Light Horse, commanded by HRH the Duke of Cumberland' and depicting the handsome figure of a light dragoon, mounted on a snorting dashing steed and brandishing a glittering sabre. Another poster declared:

The Old Saucy 'Seventh' of Queen's Own Regiment of Light Dragoons, Commanded by that gallant and well known Hero, Lieut. General Henry Lord Paget. Young fellows whose hearts beat high to tread to Paths of Glory, would not have better opportunity than now offers . . . A few smart lads will be taken at 16 years of age, 5 feet 2 inches, but they must be active and well limbed. Apply to Sergeant Hooker, Nags Head, Norwich . . .

Sir Arthur Wellesley's men were anxious to be away from their stinking, cramped quarters on the transport vessels; ahead lay the shores of a strange country and a new experience. In all the memoirs written by those who took part in the campaign there is an astonishing absence of reference to one emotion – fear, even in battle, despite the ghastly injuries which might be suffered, and not only as a result of direct armed conflict. Spain was to become notorious for scorpions: men had to have arms and legs cut off

First British troops land at Mondego Bay, July 1808, and the multitude of stores begins to pile up on the beaches.

21

when stings festered in the heat; other men died in agony from
dysentery after the normal cure of opium pills and thick rice water
had failed to have beneficial effect. But such horrors seemed far
away as the men lined the gunwales of the ships, waiting their turn
in the boats. The sun shone on the brilliant uniforms: camouflage

Young British army officers wearing resplendent, and not always practical, uniforms, often designed by their commanding officers.

colours were unheard of, and would anyway have been of minimal value in the short-range fighting which then took place, and the British redcoat was still famous. Distinctive clothing enabled commanders to identify regiments, and allowed men to sort themselves out from the enemy. British cavalry horses could be 23

Part of an officer's
baggage, even including
candlesticks and snuffer.

recognised from the French because they had their tails cut short:
a useful practice but also cruel – the animals were unable to give
themselves proper protection from tormenting flies. Officers, who
had paid for their commissions, were usually gorgeously dressed,
and the sumptuous baggage of one young nobleman was by no
means untypical: '1 Regimental Jacket; wings and lace; 2 grey
trousers; white, coloured & flannel waistcoats; flannel drawers;
12 stockings, 6 shirts, 1 pelisse; 3 prs. boots, 1 shoes . . .' Equipment
for the ordinary soldier usually consisted merely of two plain
packs – the waterproof French knapsack of unshorn goat-skin
was looked upon with envy – and the basic weapons. Most

24

Joseph Bonaparte, elder
brother of Napoleon,
was appointed King of
Spain in 1808. During
the five years of his
stormy Spanish reign he
would have to quit his
capital three times. He
eventually fled to
France, Switzerland,
and, after Waterloo, to
America. He died in
Florence in 1844, aged
76.

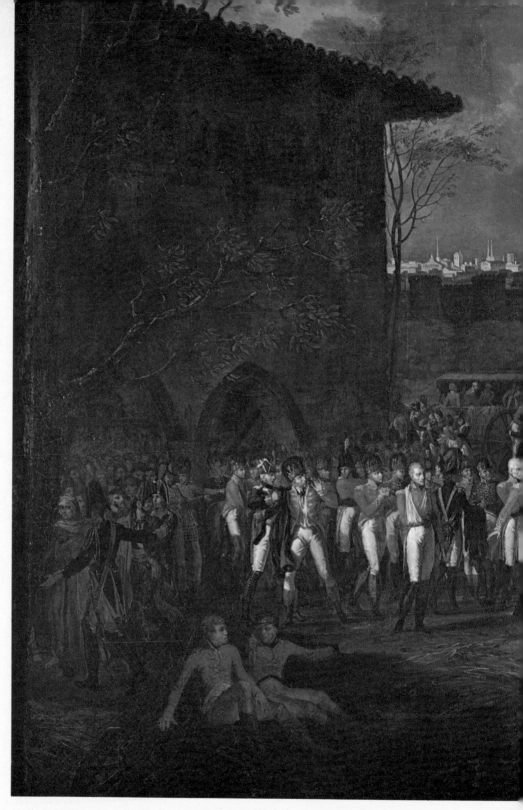

Napoleon only spent two months in Spain, and his decision to leave the fighting to his generals proved to be fatally mistaken. During his brief appearance, from 5 November 1808, to 1 January 1809, he took Madrid, then hurried north against Sir John Moore, seizing—as this painting shows—British prisoners on the way.

*Top* Battle of Rolica, 16 August 1808—the first battle of the Peninsular War. Wellesley (Wellington) had more men than his French opponent, La Borde, but not all the allied units were engaged, and the British commander laboured under the disadvantage of the threat of early French reinforcements.

*Bottom* Vimiero, 21 August 1808—Wellesley's first conclusive victory against the French, fought around the hills close by the Atlantic coast.

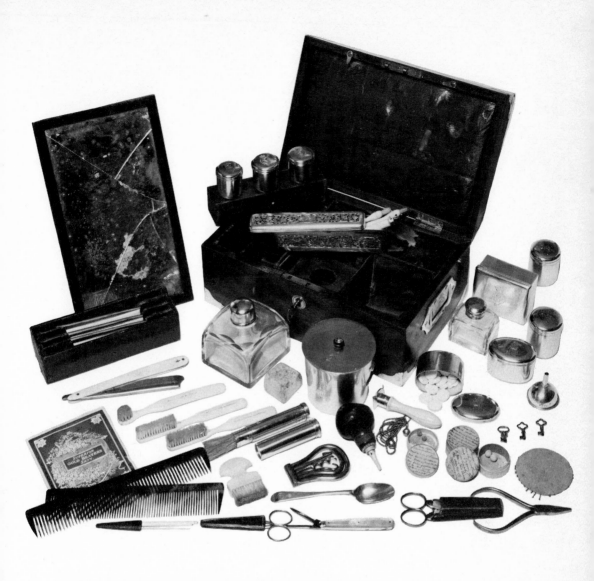

infantrymen still had muskets, rather than rifles; muskets were of the heavy 'East India' pattern, a modification of the old 'Brown Bess', smooth-bored, muzzle-loading and extremely inaccurate beyond eighty yards. Rifles were given to sharp-shooters and skirmishers, and were accurate up to about three hundred yards, but like the muskets they were prone to misfiring, needed frequent cleaning – after about thirty shots for the musket – and were even more difficult to load. This operation had to be accomplished standing up and took up to thirty seconds; a musket could be loaded and fired in half the time. French muskets were lighter but not as durable; they threw a lighter ball, and the coarse powder

Sir Arthur Wellesley's personal belongings, including pill boxes containing rhubarb and calomel tablets for purgatives.

29

used meant the barrels had to be scoured even more frequently than the British version. Musket volleys were still the most deadly form of fire, and when delivered by disciplined men firing together, each man the regulation twenty-one inches from his neighbours, they could be even more destructive than artillery.

Three kinds of standard missiles were thrown by artillery: round-shot, shells and case. The first consisted of solid iron balls which sliced through opposing forces with massive momentum; even when these balls were rolling along the ground at the end of their runs they could still tear away a man's foot or leg. Shells were lighter and usually less capable of rolling; if they did not explode in flight they lay spluttering until the fuse burnt down. Grape-shot, also known as canister or case, was used for short-range bombardments: canvas bags or other light containers were packed tight with musket balls, iron scraps or even horse-shoe nails – the bag burst open to spew the contents into the enemy ranks.

And now these guns, infantry weapons, baggage, horses, stores and men were crammed into the frail boats as Sir Arthur's army embarked for the start of the Peninsular War. The surf still swelled high. Many boats were overturned to plummet men and horses screaming into the foam. Naked sailors splashed out from the beaches to drag in boats and survivors. Sir Arthur Wellesley made the hazardous crossing early in the day and immediately began to make his dispositions. Landings in Mondego Bay would continue for another week, with Brent Spencer arriving on the 5th with his additional force. Even with these extra troops, Wellesley would not have more than 14,000 men at his disposal, and he was especially weak in cavalry and artillery, but the local Portuguese commander, Bernadino Freire, was persuaded to plan a junction with the British army at Leira, a third of the way to Lisbon. Junot had about 20,000 men, of whom about 17,000 would be available for the direct defence of the Portuguese capital.

'People of Portugal,' declared a proclamation issued by Wellesley on 2 August, 'the Time is arrived to rescue your Country; and to restore the Government of your Lawful Prince.' Eight days later the British army struck camp and took the road towards the French. Almost immediately the cruel campaigning conditions made themselves felt. The march to Leira took only twenty-four hours, but the troops were still soft from the sea voyage, and the deep sand, broiling sun, flies and heavy equipment made many men flop out of line. Bur Sir Arthur Wellesley pressed on: Leira had to be reached before French troops, thrusting by forced marches north from Lisbon under General de La Borde and west

The Baker rifle, similar to those used in the Peninsula fighting and accurate up to about 300 yards.

Wellington's first units move inland from Mondego. Within hours the raw British army experienced the harsh campaigning conditions.

Light infantry sabre, *c.* 1810, designed for hand-to-hand cutting and slashing.

from the Spanish frontier under Loison. Wellesley gained the advantage: Leira was entered and a junction prevented between the French armies at this central city. Wellesley planned to push on against La Borde and Lisbon before Loison could arrive. Almost immediately, he found that the Portuguese troops would be unable to give maximum assistance: Freire wanted the British to supply his men in addition to Wellesley's force, and, as this was impossible, Wellesley could only take 1,700 Portuguese with the main army. He headed south, reaching Alcobaça on the 14th. Next day the first British–French engagement of the Peninsular War took place outside the village of Obidos, when a detachment of the 95th Rifles clashed with French picquets. The following morning, Wellesley entered Obidos, and the French moved into positions on the far side of the village: La Borde had decided to make a stand, partly to avoid uncovering the road to Lisbon, partly because he hoped Loison would be able to strike through the hills to join him on the right. Wellesley gave no time for this merger of the French forces: he threw his men forward early on the 17th in a flanking movement along Rolica ridge. La Borde realised the danger and managed to extricate himself with the loss of 600 men; British casualties totalled 474. Wellesley lacked cavalry for pursuit and feared Loison's arrival, and La Borde withdrew to the mountains at Montechnique, fifteen miles from Lisbon. Both sides had now begun to acquire respect for one another: La Borde realised his enemy commander was quick-witted and versatile; Wellesley described the French performance as 'their best style' – and he realised even more keenly the need for reinforcements.

Early next morning he learnt this need might soon be partially met. Dispatches reached his camp near Rolica, where the army was obliged to bivouac in line of battle ready for a renewed French threat, to inform him of the arrival of 4,000 British troops off the coast. Orders were immediately given for a march to the sleepy village of Vimiero, where cover could be given for the disembarkation. Troops were landed on the 18th, 19th and 20th – and on the last day Wellesley's period of freedom ended: the sloop *Brazen* carried on board Sir Harry Burrard, his superior. Wellesley brushed dust and sand from his plain grey uniform and braved the surf to go out and meet him. The interview was no better than expected.

'I don't know what Govt. propose to do with me,' Wellesley had written to his brother William on the 19th. 'I shall be the junior of all the Lt. Generals; & of all the awkward situations in the world that which is most so is, to serve in a subordinate capacity in an

Army which one has commanded . . . I think they had better order me home.' Despite this pessimism, Wellesley stooped into the master cabin on board the *Brazen* determined to state his case. Junot had left Lisbon, and would take advantage of the delay caused by the extra British disembarkation; Wellesley therefore outlined a typically bold scheme to Burrard: the army should advance south as soon as possible and outflank the French. The cautious Burrard disagreed: the British would be outnumbered, he claimed, despite the latest arrivals, and he ordered a delay until Sir John Moore's men had reached Portugal.

But Junot himself was not prepared to wait for British strength to be further swollen. He ordered a thrust north from Torres Vedras on the evening of the 20th, even as Wellesley and Burrard argued on board the *Brazen*. Bad roads prevented the French arrival near the British positions at Vimiero until the early morning on the 21st. Meanwhile, as Sir Harry Burrard spent another leisurely night afloat, Wellesley hurriedly threw his men into line to face the

The Battle of Rolica seen from the French positions: British troops advance at close range whilst others, in the middle distance, threaten a flanking movement. *From* Martial Achievements, *drawn by W. Heath, engraved by T. Sutherland.*

33

Vimiero: Sir Arthur Wellesley sends fresh orders to the British lines after the first French assault has been repulsed.

expected threat from the south. At 9 am clouds of distant dust indicated the approach of the French army – but from an unexpected direction: the east. Aides were rushed with fresh orders from Wellesley's HQ on the ridge along the Maceira river;

sweating and swearing troops ran to new positions as the British

commander took urgent steps to avoid this left flanking movement.
For a while pandemonium seemed to settle over the British army:
units were wheeling, marching, scurrying; dust hung heavy in
the hot air, churned by thousands of feet; shouts and commands
mingled with the screeching of ammunition carts and the neighing

of horses. Wellesley remained outwardly cool. Sir Harry was still at sea.

Two ridges run inland at right angles from the sea in the Vimiero area. The Maceira river runs through a gorge just to the north of the western ridge, then bends south between the two lines of hills. Vimiero village lies near this gap, and just to the south of the village is a lower rise, known as Vimiero hill. The British army was originally concentrated on and around the western ridge to protect the landings from a southern advance: on the night of the 20th five of the eight brigades were in this area, only two were on Vimiero hill, and the remaining few troops were further east. This southern emphasis was switched by moving three brigades from the west to the far tip of the eastern ridge: Ferguson's, Nightingall's and Bowe's. Another brigade, Acland's, hurried to the western end of this rise overlooking the village. Crauford's brigade joined Trant's Portuguese troops to the north of the region. Only Hill's brigade remained on the western ridge, while the remainder of the army were positioned on Vimiero hill. The bulk of the army was therefore concentrated on the eastern rise, with the right flank on Vimiero hill and the left in the broken country to the north. Final preparations were still being made as the French advanced. Few enemy troops could be seen in the hummocky, wooded terrain; instead the line of march could be identified by the rising cloud of dust. Junot was evidently pushing his men forward in three columns: one was continuing northwards, possibly in an attempt to turn the British left flank; another was moving north-west towards Ferguson's brigade at the end of the east ridge; the third seemed to be striking west towards Vimiero hill, and the latter, with the shortest distance to cover, would plainly arrive first.

The French were renowned for their skirmisher troops: these *tirailleurs* would swarm in front of the main columns, firing from individual cover to confuse and weaken the opposing lines. Following them would come the solid infantry formations, to smash into the flustered enemy forces. This Napoleonic practice had worked well, especially against the rigid, unimaginative and inflexible Prussian lines at Jena and Auerstadt, where troops had had to stand unprotected as perfect targets. Sir Arthur Wellesley had already thought out an answer to the problem. First, he threw forward a British skirmishing line to match the French; this, comprising over half Fane's brigade, was deployed about 800 yards in front of Vimiero hill, armed with rifles and making full use of available cover. Remaining troops on the hill, five battalions, were positioned in cover just over the crest, or even further back in support. Twelve guns were to give added firepower.

The black mass of French infantry emerged from the gullies and woods; and almost immediately Wellesley's guess at the enemy tactics was confirmed. Troops advancing upon Vimiero hill split into two columns, one moving towards the slope in the centre, the second further to the south-east, and in front ran the *tirailleurs*; field artillery moved with the columns while cavalry trotted at the flanks. British skirmishers met the French with deadly frontal fire. Crackling rifles merged into a steady staccato drumming like heavy rain on a tin roof. French skirmishers hesitated, fell, moved back; only the brave survivors went on – to be met by thrusting British bayonets. Up stepped the main British lines from behind the crest to pour rolling musket-fire into the enemy columns, with the Britishers standing only two deep to allow both ranks to fire unobstructed. The thudding roar of the guns echoed down into the long, smoking valley. The French suffered from the new British tactics, and also from a new weapon – shrapnel, invented in 1785 by the man who gave his name to this deadly, exploding shell, and now used for the first time on any large scale. The French columns, weakened and bleeding, courageously came forward four times; their lines lapped around the base of the hill; British troops were forced to give ground, but each time the French were pushed back again with terrible losses. Sir Harry Burrard puffed up to the battle during these charges; somewhat superfluously he gave Sir Arthur Wellesley permission to continue the battle.

During the confusion of the fourth attack on the hill a French grenadier brigade veered northwards towards Vimiero village, keeping to low ground. No British troops stood directly in their way. The thrust threatened to slice between the main British positions, but Wellesley realised the danger: four companies from Acland's brigade were ordered down from the east ridge to fire upon the French at close range, while Fane's men on Vimiero hill gave similar enfilade fire from the south; Anstruther sent soldiers from his second line, positioned behind Vimiero hill, into the village itself. The French grenadiers pushed into the houses despite terrible fire into their flanks, and vicious hand-to-hand fighting took place in the narrow, stone-walled streets, with the British outnumbered about three to two. But the French feared being cut off and gradually retreated, again suffering from flank fire.

Wellesley believed the battle was starting to flow in his favour and tried to hurry the tide along. Colonel Taylor's 20th Light Dragoons were ordered to charge the reeling French lines near

Vimiero hill. The result was disastrous. Portuguese horsemen lost heart and soon came back, while British dragoons plunged on at full gallop completely out of control and outside artillery support, and Taylor and most of his men were shot or hacked down. Meanwhile, fighting was fast developing on the eastern ridge, where Wellesley himself was situated. One French column had continued northwards, towards Trant and Crauford: this was allowed to continue. Another column of about 3,000 men turned west at the village of Ventosa and struck towards Ferguson's position on the ridge. The main British lines were again in cover behind the crest, and skirmishers were deployed on the slopes facing the French. The enemy, commanded by General Solignac, were in a vastly disadvantageous position: *tirailleurs* had to force their way uphill against the British skirmishers, and sought support from their main infantry lines. Gradually they struggled up the slope; the British riflemen pulled back. Then, when the French were less than a hundred yards from the summit, the main British lines advanced from the other side. A sudden, unexpected and murderous close-range fire riddled the French; the enemy were superior in number but only the heads of their platoons could fire, while the full British volleys split the massed French ranks. Solignac's attempts to re-form his men from column into extended line only caused further confusion. After only two terrible minutes – ten British volleys – the formations had been blown apart and sent reeling down the hill, and Ferguson moved forward ready to cut Solignac's survivors from the main French army in the south. Another enemy attack by troops under General Brennier met with similar disaster; Brennier himself was captured and immediately questioned by Wellesley.

The British commander knew he had the French almost on the run. The hour was only noon; half a day of fighting and slaughter still remained. No French reserves were left; most French ranks were shattered; French morale had slumped. Now was the time for the British counter-attack – and the troops realised this almost as much as Wellesley himself. Fane and Anstruther had to restrain their stamping, shouting, swearing infantrymen. 'Charge!' shouted the men. 'Damn it! Tell us to charge, damn you!' Wellesley put spurs to his sweating horse and thundered up to Sir Harry Burrard, theoretically in charge of the British army. 'Sir Harry, now is your chance,' shouted Wellesley. 'The French are completely beat; we have a large body of troops that have not yet been in action. Let us move on Torres Vedras. You take the force here straight forward; I will bring round the left with the troops

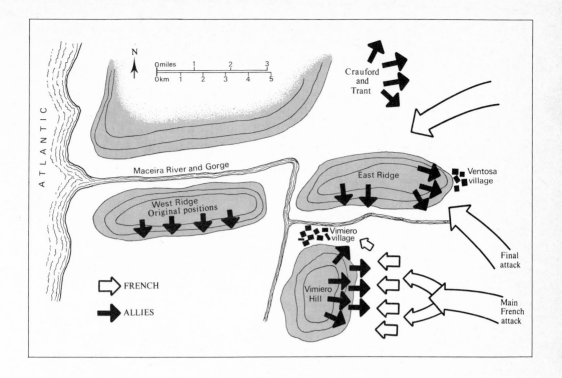

In the map:

N

0 miles 1 2 3
0 km 1 2 3 4 5

Craford
and
Trant

A T L A N T I C

Maceira River and Gorge

East Ridge

Ventosa village

West Ridge
Original positions

Vimiero village

Final attack

FRENCH

ALLIES

Vimiero
Hill

Main
French
attack

already there. We'll be in Lisbon in three days!'

An hour or so earlier, Sir Harry had had little choice over allowing the fighting to continue. Now, with Sir Arthur Wellesley's confirmation that the French were beaten, he had. And he immediately reverted to the opinion held the previous day: it would be best to await the arrival of Sir John Moore's contingent; and the army had done enough for one day. Troops must now go back to their bivouacs; even the French trapped by Ferguson should be allowed to escape. Wellesley reined his horse away in disgust. His staff followed him, and heard him snarl that they might as well enjoy themselves shooting red partridge.

The plain east and south of Vimiero was littered with bodies, crawling wounded and bewildered stragglers. Groups of soldiers, French and British, helped maimed men back to their respective sides. Surviving French lines were regrouped and the dust of their retreat dwindled away over the horizon. The sun set red. Despite efforts of clearing parties, the screams and moans of the wounded still sounded from the battlefield during the hot, sticky night. As many as possible of the maimed were carted from the field to the rough operating tables set up in the nearby scrub. And there the surgeons undertook their grisly work throughout the hours of

Map 1   The Battle of Vimiero.

darkness, the tables lit by yellow lamps around which fluttered huge black moths. About the surgeons were strewn the tools of their trade: tourniquets, forceps, scalpels, saws and glittering sharp knives – the latter were always in great domestic demand as second-hand meat carvers. Heaped by the tables were untidy and increasingly bloody piles of lint, tow, sponges, splints, ready-coated adhesive plaster and cards of thread. Surgery itself was simple. Chest or abdominal wounds were merely stitched up or plastered over, regardless of the havoc inside the wound itself; probing was done with bloody bare fingers to find embedded missiles, although musket balls were removed by specially shaped forceps. As for the rest, and apart from simple fractures and bandaging, surgery consisted of amputation. No time could be spared for cleaning and treating shattered arms or legs and time would anyway probably have been wasted: round shot and sabre thrusts caused such terrible damage that any less drastic treatment would have been useless. So limbs were lopped off – without antiseptics or anaesthetics: wine and diluted rum were used only to strengthen patients, rather than to render them insensible. An astonishing number of troops managed to survive, and they were probably helped by the practice which became increasingly common during the Peninsular War: an argument had long taken place over the best time to perform the amputation – as soon as possible, or two or three days later when the patient had recovered from shock, or a number of weeks later when the patient was as rested and ready as ever he would be. Surgeons in Spain adopted the first method: patients were brought straight from the field to the operating boards and their limbs were sawn off almost immediately. Only later would improved medical science confirm that this was, in fact, the best procedure.

The sun beat down upon the dead and dying next morning, 22 August, and the vultures swarmed like the flies. The stench was appalling. Yet humour could still penetrate this horror. British troops watched fascinated as one major rode backwards and forwards across the battlefield, his sweating horse picking a delicate way through the debris; the major, well-known for his bravery, had previously worn long flowing hair to compensate for his ugly features, but now the astonished soldiers saw his head was bald, his bare pate already burnt red by the sun. 'A guinea,' he kept crying 'a guinea to any man who will find my wig.'

Sir Hew Dalrymple, British Commander-in-Chief, had arrived by sea late the previous evening but had still to come ashore, and Sir Arthur Wellesley exerted pressure on Burrard to change his mind over pursuit of the French. At the same time he penned a letter to Lord Castlereagh: 'I believe he (Burrard) will march tomorrow. Indeed, if he does not, we shall be poisoned here by the stench of the dead and wounded; or we shall starve, everything in the neighbourhood being already eaten up.' But disappointment soon multiplied. Although Wellesley remained *de facto* commander of the army – he wrote to his brother William on the 22nd: 'I still command the Army; as all Heads of Department won't go to anybody else' – his superiors nevertheless had the final word over strategy. Sir Hew Dalrymple stepped onshore during the day and proved even more obstinate than Burrard. No pursuit. Arguments raged in the British camp during that afternoon, to no avail. The angry debate still continued when an alarm was raised: French cavalry were approaching. But British spy-glasses soon made out a fluttering white flag: the horsemen trotted into the British lines, led by General Kellerman whose ugly face was made even more sinister by the assorted black sticking-plaster freely placed upon it. Junot had realised he must accept temporary defeat, yet the lack of British pursuit had also convinced him that, miraculously, he might be able to negotiate an escape for his army. Kellerman therefore brought an offer from his commander: the French were willing to depart from Portugal – if British vessels were used for transportation. A 48-hour truce should be observed to work out details. A truce was arranged, and the terms of a convention drawn up. These were ratified on 31 August by Sir Hew at Torres Vedras and by Junot at Lisbon; on 1 September the British HQ moved to Cintra, nearer Lisbon, and the agreement thereafter became known as the Convention of Cintra. The French gave up intact all forts, arsenals, weapons and military stores, including the powerful border fortress towns of Elvas and Almeida; enemy troops were to sail to France in British ships – but no time was specified for their abstinence from further hostilities. Such a restriction would anyway have been impossible to supervise. Wellesley had no choice but to sign the document – he was so ordered by Sir Hew – and, as he wrote to his brother William on 24 August, he was by no means against the controversial Convention as a whole, under the existing difficult circumstances.

I approve of allowing the French to withdraw from Portugal, because Sir Harry Burrard and Sir Hew Dalrymple would not, or could not carry into execution the plan of operations for Sir John Moore's corps which I had proposed to Sir Harry, according to which it would have been placed at Santarem & would have cut off the retreat of the French to Elvas; & therefore the convention is necessary in order to set the British troops at liberty to go into Spain at an early period of the year.

Sir Arthur did however disagree with the indefinite term given to the suspension of hostilities, and also believed measures should be taken 'to force the French Generals to disgorge some of the Church Plate which they have stolen'.

Shock and disgust swept through Portugal over the Convention, and fierce opposition arose in Britain when the terms were published in the *London Gazette* on 16 September, despite the fact that the agreement achieved, without further bloodshed, the British aim of clearing the French from Portugal. Both Wordsworth and Byron took up their poetic pens to denounce the document, and before long the Tory ministry would be forced to institute a court of inquiry, calling before it Dalrymple and Burrard and involving Sir Arthur Wellesley. The latter was heartily sick of the whole business long before this outcry found full voice. 'I wish that I was away from this Army,' he complained to his brother on 25 August. 'Things will not flourish as we are situated, & organised; & I am much afraid that my friends in England will consider me responsible for many things over which I have no power.' Wellesley had urged the landing of Sir John Moore's troops further north to cut off a possible French retreat, but even before the Convention received ratification his superiors had decided that these latest arrivals should beach in Maceira Bay. Moore's contingent accordingly arrived at the end of August.

There were soldiers, horses, sailors [wrote one eye-witness at the disembarkation], guns, wagons, some of which were being fitted together, mountains of ship's biscuits, haversacks, trusses of hay, barrels of meat and rum . . . dragoons busy catching and saddling their horses. But the latter could not be mounted for, owing to their long sojourn in the ship, during which they had been standing, they had lost the use of the legs, and the moment a trooper mounted one of them, the horse folded up.

Sir John Moore came ashore on the 24th, assisted by Captain Bligh of HMS *Alfred*. From Bligh and General Crauford he heard the full story of the Battle of Vimiero and of Wellesley's insistence that the enemy should be pursued. 'Sir Arthur's views . . . were extremely right,' noted Moore, and a message of congratulation was immediately sent to the victorious commander. The following evening a reply came back. 'I wish you had arrived a few days sooner . . . But you are not now too late, and I hope you will soon come to headquarters and ascertain the state and means of this army, and state your opinion to the Commander-in-Chief respecting the means to be adopted.' Wellesley warned that winter weather would soon set in and added: 'We have done nothing since the 21st.' Later that night Moore reached headquarters;

Wellesley was not present, and the newcomer was disturbed to find 'the greatest confusion and a very general discontent'.

Wellesley's own discontent was increasing by the hour. 'If I could be of any use to men who have served me so well,' he wrote on the evening of the 29th, 'I would stay with them for ever; but as matters are situated, I am sure that I can be of no use to them . . . I have determined to go home immediately.' This determination was repeated in a letter to Castlereagh the following day. 'Matters are not prospering here; and I feel an earnest desire to quit the army.' Five days later the feeling had grown even stronger. 'It is quite impossible,' he warned the Secretary of War, 'for me to continue any longer with this army.' 'I am sick of the state of public affairs,' he added to William next day. The following afternoon, 7 September, Sir John Moore called upon Sir Hew Dalrymple. The Commander-in-Chief had received a dispatch from Lord Castlereagh which suggested future operations in Spain 'upon the flank and rear, as he called it, of the French from Santander or Gijon, whilst the Spanish pressed them in front.' Sir John Moore commented privately: 'This is a sort of gibberish which men in office use and fancy themselves military men.' Publicly, he warned Sir Hew that until contact had been made with leading Spanish officials no plans should, or even could, be made. Sir Hew replied that he did not even know who the leading Spanish generals would be. A number of possible names were mentioned, including General Castaños, said to have a very neatly powdered head and to be a stickler for etiquette, his rival Cuesta, and the unknown Llamas; others included General Palafox, only twenty-eight and with no military experience but very popular, and General Joachim Blake, a colourful Irish mercenary. Sir John Moore left the interview feeling considerable and justifiable unease. Further, he knew that negotiations over the mechanics of the Cintra Convention were moving far too slowly: the French were proving difficult to deal with over details of fortress evacuation, and the Portuguese were being obstructive. Moore visited Lisbon on the 9th. Confusion was rampant in the capital: the police had been disbanded, public services had broken down, and the Portuguese were rioting over the Cintra Convention – newspaper items on the agreement were printed inside a thick black border of mourning. Relations between the British, French and Portuguese were tense; civilians were refusing to feed Junot's men, and Junot and his officers were stuffing their baggage with bizarre items of 'personal belongings' including valuable medieval manuscripts, sacred paintings and, as Wellesley had warned, precious Church plate. Moore was sick of 43

the capital within a few hours and learnt with relief that his division was to move to Queluz, not far from the city, where Moore would establish his HQ in the pretty pink palace. Moore arrived at Queluz on 17 September and found an astonishing letter awaiting him.

Wellesley had continued to fret over the army command. So too had Moore, writing in his private journal that he believed the two present Chiefs must soon be relieved: 'To whom the command will then be given, I cannot guess. Something very brilliant will be given to Sir Arthur.' Sir Arthur Wellesley himself had different ideas, which he outlined in his letter to Moore at Queluz on the 17th. 'It appears to me to be quite impossible that we can go on as we are now constituted; the Commander-in-Chief must be

Well satisfied with the negotiations, Junot leaves Lisbon under the terms of the Cintra Convention. Junot died four years later.

changed, and the country and the army naturally turn their eyes to you.' The victor of Vimiero then referred to the upset between Moore and the ministers after the general's precipitous return from Sweden. 'I understand . . . that you have lately had some unpleasant discussions . . . the effect of which might be to prevent the adoption of an arrangement for the command of this army.' Wellesley offered himself as go-between:

I wish you would allow me to talk to you respecting the discussions to which I have averted, in order that I may endeavour to remove any trace which they may have left on the minds of the King's Ministers . . . I am no party man; but have long been connected in friendship with many of those persons who are now at the head of affairs in England; and I think I have sufficient influence over them . . .

45

The note was potentially explosive. From the lines wafted the smell of intrigue, and with Moore already out of favour any suggestion of surreptitious dealing could be personally disastrous. 'This letter surprised me,' wrote Sir John Moore in his journal, 'as I have little previous acquaintance with Sir Arthur, and have had very little communication with him since I joined this army.' Nevertheless, Moore was curious, and he too was concerned over the army command. He sent a note inviting Wellesley to Queluz; the following afternoon, 18 September, Wellesley's horse cantered up to the pink palace and he strode briskly into Moore's room.

His face – almost blackened by the sun – was stern and unforgiving, and his grey-blue eyes were even colder than usual. He looked almost Spanish, especially in contrast to Moore's Scottish fairness. Almost immediately he embarked on a long denunciation of the present commanders – 'the Dowager Dalrymple and Betty Burrard' – before revealing he had asked for leave and would sail home the following day, inferring that once·in London he would press for drastic alterations. Moore gave a cautious and even cool answer: he agreed with some points made by Wellesley and he himself felt his position to be difficult. He wished he had never been chosen for his present appointment. 'But it is the business of Government to remove me if they think proper . . . I can enter into no intrigue.' 'In these times, my dear General,' insisted Wellesley, 'a man like you should not preclude himself from rendering the services of which he is capable, by an idle point of form.'

Sir Arthur Wellesley sailed for Plymouth the following day, and would arrive on 4 October. On the day he reached home, Sir Hew Dalrymple left for England on the *Phoebe*. The outcry against the Cintra Convention had reached its height in London; Sir Hew had been summoned to explain himself, being directed to resign the command to the officer next in line. Sir Harry Burrard believed himself equally implicated and decided to depart a few days later. Wellesley reached London on 5 October: 'I don't know whether I am to be hanged, drawn and quartered; or roasted alive.' Presumably he still intended to smooth over the misunderstanding between Moore and the Government, but his scheme was already outdated: his ship to England had crossed a fast frigate heading for Portugal with instructions from Downing Street, addressed to Lieutenant-General Sir John Moore and dated 25 September. Sir John opened these orders on 6 October.

Sir, His Majesty having determined to employ a corps of his troops, of not less than 30,000 infantry and 5,000 cavalry, in the North of Spain, to cooperate with the Spanish armies in the expulsion of the French from that Kingdom, has been graciously pleased to entrust to you the Command in Chief of this Force.

Moore was highly elated. 'They have given me . . . the greatest command that any English general has had this century. I hope I may be able to acquit myself as becomes me.'

But with this elation went a sober realisation of immense difficulties involved. The plan for a move into Spain was popular, both with officers and men: gruff General Beresford, commander in Lisbon, had already commented: 'We do not understand rotting here while our friends the Spaniards are, with such earnestness, demanding our assistance.' Nevertheless, such assistance was easy to promise yet infinitely more difficult to give. The troops had indeed been rotting. Cold weather was already setting in, made more harsh by the contrast with the sweltering summer campaign. Sickness was steadily increasing; morale was low; troops grumbled about the inactivity and about the local squalor and the apparent unwillingness of the Portuguese to help the British with the fighting.

The grand object at present [replied Moore to Castlereagh], is to get the troops out of Portugal before the rains set in; but, at this instant, the army is without equipment of any kind, either for the carriage of the light baggage of regiments, artillery stores, Commissariat stores, or other appendages of an army; and not a magazine is formed in any of the routes by which we are to march.

Moore added:

I mention this circumstance in the first place, because it is a truth, and in the next to prevent your Lordship from being too sanguine as to the probable period of my reaching the North of Spain.

Moore had been left a depressing legacy: grossly inadequate preparations, a disastrous delay in deciding upon this expedition to Spain, and now the need for all speed before the winter. The new British commander hurriedly planned how best to carry out his hazardous mission. First, he shifted the emphasis given in the orders sent from London: instead of the 'North of Spain' he selected targets further south in the central Spanish region, and specifically the important towns of Almeida and Ciudad Rodrigo. To reach north Spain the army would have had to be transported to Corunna by sea, in order to reach the area before winter, but the year was already so far advanced that such a sea passage would have been uncertain. Moreover, he had been told by Castlereagh that rein-forcements were being sent to him from England under Sir David Baird, amounting to 10,000 men; these would land at Corunna and the countryside around the port would not provide sufficient resources for both Baird's force and his own. Finally, Spanish 47 generals with whom contact had now been made strongly recommended Almeida and Ciudad Rodrigo. An overland march would therefore be attempted in this direction; informing Castlereagh of his intentions, Moore added that Sir Harry Burrard agreed with the scheme and had proved most cooperative.

No time could be wasted and, as if to underline the need for speed, chill winds swept up from the Tagus and through the Lisbon streets and rain splattered on the curved tile roofs. On 9 October, only three days after receiving his instructions from London, Moore issued a General Order to his army.

The Troops under Lieutenant-General Sir John Moore will hold themselves in readiness to move on the shortest notice . . . All heavy baggage will be left in Lisbon . . . Directions will be given with respect to the sick. The Lieutenant-General sees with much concern the great number of this description and that it daily increases. The General assures the troops that it is owing to their own intemperance that so many of them are rendered incapable of marching against the enemy.

Even harder than giving up the cheap Portuguese wine was the next sacrifice which the troops were called upon to suffer – abandonment of women. A further order was issued next day, 10 October.

As in the course of the long march which the army is about to undertake, and where no carts will be allowed, the women would unavoidably be exposed to the greatest hardship and distress, commanding officers are therefore desired to use their endeavours to prevent as many as possible . . . from following the army. Those who remain will be left with the heavy baggage.

The number of women had been severely reduced before the original departure from London – six to every one hundred men, drawn by lot. This still gave a sizeable female contingent, and despite Moore's latest edict, many still managed to slip after the troops. Few would survive.

A solitary drum beat a steady tattoo on the morning of Tuesday, 11 October 1808, and the first troops filed from Queluz camp on the start of the fateful march towards the Spanish border. Despite recent rain the dust soon billowed high above the beaten track as regiment followed regiment; some men sang; the ubiquitous oxen-carts screeched and scraped; mules brayed, chickens clucked, artillery carriages creaked, and always the steady pulsating of the drums. 'The regiments are already marching,' wrote Moore to a lady friend in London. 'As soon as I have seen everything in train here, I shall push on and get to their head. Pray for good weather; if it rains the torrents will swell, and be impassable, and I shall be accounted a bungler . . .'

48

The general also wrote: 'Upon the whole, if we get over this march, nothing after will appear difficult.' His main force, totalling 20,000 men, had to be split into two, owing to the belief – mistaken as it happened – that no artillery road existed between Lisbon and Almeida. Moore therefore sent most of his guns along a longer southern route, screened by cavalry and some infantry, under the command of Sir John Hope. Moore himself travelled with the bulk of the army, leaving Lisbon on 27 October. The other section of his forces, Baird's 10,000, had started to land at Corunna on the 12th. Moore planned that the three parts – Baird advancing from Corunna, Hope via Badajoz, and his own via Almeida – would merge at Salamanca or even Burgos, prior to a concentration at Valladolid. The separate movements would have been complicated under any circumstances; they were made doubly difficult by the absence of maps, by the inadequacies of Portuguese guides, and the lack of time.

The difficulties attending the subsistence of the troops through Portugal [wrote Moore to Lord Bentinck], are greater than you would believe. The information respecting roads should have been got, and the arrangements for supplies should have been made, before the troops began to march. But when I got the command nothing of this sort had been done. They talked of going into Spain as going into Hyde Park.

Only one factor seemed in his favour: the French still seemed inactive behind the Ebro river, commanded by Marshal Jean Jourdan since 25 August. But Moore knew that when they moved from their defensive positions he would be critically outnumbered – about 70,000 to his 30,000. The deficit would be to some extent made up by Spanish support, but as Moore advanced towards the frontier he became increasingly apprehensive over future Anglo-Spanish relations. Spain was governed through a system of local bodies, Juntas, theoretically subject to the 32-man Central Junta in Madrid, but in practice often swayed by provincial motives. Before leaving Lisbon, Moore had heard that the disembarkation of Baird's force at Corunna had been hindered by the temporary refusal of the Galicia Junta to give landing permission: the incident gave an indication of future complications. What, for example, was Sir John Moore's seniority position in relation to the top Spanish military commander – whoever he might be? Lord William Bentinck was dispatched to Madrid in an attempt to clarify the situation. Meanwhile, Moore crossed the Tagus at Villa Velha on 3 November. So far roads had been reasonably good, although the surrounding countryside had been gloomy and desolate. On 5 November, between Castello Branco and Alpedrinha, Moore received a sombre dispatch from Bentinck. General Francesco de Castaños, lucky victor over Dupont at Baylen on 23 July, was deemed to be the senior Spanish general, and had apparently taken the field with the Aragon army, but the French seemed to be moving on to the offensive and had been reinforced by 10,000 men. This activity, both Spanish and French, would probably result in an action in the near future. Moore, still separated from his artillery, felt additional unease, and immediately sent a message ordering Hope to avoid Madrid and to make a junction with his main force as soon as possible. As to the question of supreme command, Bentinck reported that the Central Junta believed the British should concert their movement with General Castaños – which sounded very much like a desire for Moore to be subordinate to his Spanish counterpart.

Also on 5 November, a small, neat figure rode briskly into the French main camp. Napoleon had joined his army. And this army was receiving a massive increase – as many as 200,000 men were crowding over the Pyrenees, including veterans and men of the Old Guard from Germany. Napoleon was determined to have an end to this Spanish nonsense; his armies were ordered to strike hard, and fast. He himself would command the forces in central and southern Spain, leaving Soult in charge in the north.

Dawn, 6 November, brought a torrential downpour onto Moore's advancing units. The British commander had hoped to reach Guarda that night, but was unable to make it until the following day. His troops rested and attempted to dry sodden clothes and equipment. The advance continued on the 10th. On the same day the French broke out of the Ebro valley in full force; Napoleon entered Burgos on the 11th. Moore was unable to reach Almeida until the 13th, but he crossed the Portuguese–Spanish frontier later in the day. His original plan – a junction of his three sections at Salamanca or Burgos – was now obviously impossible: the latter city was firmly in French hands, and although Moore's main force reached Salamanca between the 13th and 23rd, Hope and the artillery would not be able to arrive until the beginning of December, and Baird was still marching over the rugged mountains from Corunna. Even Moore's main force would take a number of days to be reorganised after the long march – and within hours of his arrival at Salamanca reports confirmed the presence of French cavalry detachments at Valladolid, only six miles away. Further depressing news was rushed to the British HQ. General Joachim Blake, the Irish soldier of fortune, had suffered a reverse at Zornosa; French reinforcements were flooding into the country.

Later this day, 13 November, Moore made a sad speech to the Junta at Salamanca. He was heard in total silence. If the French advanced, he warned, no option would remain but to fall back to the frontier town of Ciudad Rodrigo – a possibility he had always envisaged if the French moved before he had had time to merge his forces. His newly arrived troops had already been ordered to prepare to march. Be calm, advised Moore.

On 14 November, the day the court of inquiry into the Cintra Convention opened in Chelsea's Great Hall, Moore heard of further setbacks. Joachim Blake had suffered more defeats near Espinosa. Only one Spanish force of any size now survived which could give the British support; this, commanded by Castaños, consisted mainly of peasantry. For the next five days Moore tried frantically to organise his men and to distribute all possible equipment; an additional difficulty was the acute shortage of ready money. He sent off urgent messages to Castaños, only to receive the belated information on the 19th that this general had been deprived of his command. And his successor, General La Romana, had apparently disappeared. 'God knows where,' despaired Moore to the British Ambassador at Madrid, Mr John Hookham Frere. 'If things are to continue in this state, the ruin of the Spanish cause and the defeat of their armies is inevitable, and it will become my duty to consider alone the safety of the British Army, and to take

General Sir John Moore's small army crosses the Tagus near Villa Velha, 3 November 1808, on the fatal mission to Spain. From a water-colour sketch by the Reverend William Bradford, Chaplain of Brigade.

51

steps to withdraw it.' A report came from Sir John Hope, making all speed to meet him: Spanish military authorities with whom Hope had been in contact had no plan of operations.

I am within four marches of the French [wrote Moore to a friend in London on the 20th], with only a third of my force; and as the Spaniards have been dispersed in all quarters, my junction with the other two thirds is very precarious; and when we all join we shall be very inferior to the enemy. The Spanish Government is weak and imbecile . . . We are in a scrape; but I hope we shall have spirit to get out of it. You must, however, be prepared to hear very bad news.

On the 26th Moore heard from Baird, whose advance troops were at Astorga, that the French were believed to be moving to prevent his junction with the main British force; on the 28th a dispatch from Hope reported that he too was convinced the enemy were moving either to prevent his link-up with Moore at Salamanca or to destroy his advance magazine. Later in the day Moore was informed that Castaños had suffered a total defeat near Tudela. Spanish forces had been scattered; the separated British forces would soon be surrounded and defeated piecemeal. Moore made the only decision which seemed open to him: late on the 28th he ordered Baird to fall back on the coast and sail for Lisbon, and Hope to be prepared to retire on Ciudad Rodrigo. Moore summoned his officers to inform them of his plan next morning: faces were long and considerable opposition was expressed to this idea of withdrawal. Moore would not allow argument, but at the same time would not move his force just yet; he still hoped Hope might be able to slip through and join him, especially if French attention was diverted by the mistaken belief that the British main force had already retired from Salamanca.

British troops were ready to march at instant notice, but for the moment they remained at Salamanca. Meanwhile intense pressure was put upon Moore to change his mind and move against the French. The Spanish opinion was vehemently voiced by Ambassador Frere in Madrid: retreat would have a disastrous effect on Spanish morale. 'It would sink the hearts of the whole country.' Nor was Moore himself so convinced as he had sounded when addressing his officers: militarily, the decision to withdraw was the only choice; politically, there might be something to be said for a sacrifice to help the Spaniards. Moreover, a spirit of resistance now appeared to be rising in Madrid. And on 4 December Sir John Hope's division reached Alba de Tormes, only fifteen miles from Salamanca. On the 5th, Moore received another urgent message from Frere. 'I consider the fate of Spain as depending absolutely,

*Opposite page* General Sir John Moore. Aged 47 at the start of the Peninsular War and, with Wellesley, considered the most able of Britain's field commanders, Sir John was shadowed by criticism of his handling of his previous assignment. And now, in Spain, Moore had to carry out ill-conceived, inadequate and dangerous instructions from London. *From the portrait by T. Lawrence*

52

Lord Henry William Paget, perhaps the most skilful British cavalry officer in the Napoleonic Wars. Paget's time in the Peninsular was however brief: in spring, 1809, he eloped with the wife of Wellington's brother, Henry, and this family scandal ruled out service with the British commander. By 1815 all had been forgotten: Paget commanded the British cavalry at Waterloo. *From the painting by T. Lawrence*

for the present, upon the decision which you may adopt.' A new Junta had been formed for the defence of Madrid, headed by the Duke of Infantado, who wanted Moore to assume chief command of all Spanish forces. 'Madrid would resist the invaders.' Sir John Moore paced his candle-lit chamber – and changed his mind over retreat; during the night he scratched out a message to Baird, describing the plans for resistance in the Spanish capital.

I must beg therefore that you will suspend your march until you hear from me again, and make arrangements for your return to Astorga . . . All this appears very strange and unsteady, but if the spirit of enthusiasm does arise in Spain, and the people will be martyrs, there is no saying, in that case, what our force may do . . . If the bubble bursts, and Madrid falls, we shall have a run for it.

Frere's letter describing the Madrid resistance had been dated 2 December, four days before. A rising had indeed broken out on 2 December. Within forty-eight hours it had been crushed and the capital had surrendered. Even as Sir John Moore decided to postpone plans for a safe withdrawal in order to help Madrid's resistance, the French were in full occupation of the city.

This distressing news was not received by Moore until the 9th. Now it made no difference to his new plans – which were amongst the most daring and brilliant of the entire Peninsular War. Moore was hopelessly outnumbered by as many as ten to one and the enemy were commanded by Napoleon himself; but the British had one possible advantage: surprise. Intelligence reports indicated Napoleon was unsure of Moore's whereabouts but thought the British were withdrawing, and the French were therefore moving south on Andalusia and not Salamanca, which was believed already abandoned. Moore therefore decided to strike in the opposite direction, north-east towards the river Douro and even towards Burgos. If he moved quickly enough, without even waiting for Baird, the French would be caught off-balance and would have to pull back from their southward march in order to protect communications. Enemy forces would thus be drawn away from the Spaniards, who might be able to use the breathing space to reorganise and strike back. 'I was aware that I was risking infinitely too much,' wrote Moore, 'but something must be risked for the honour of the Service.' The danger was indeed great: when the British finally withdrew, as they would have to do, the French would be hard on their heels.

Moore's army slipped from Salamanca on the 12th and 13th. On 14 December the British commander established his headquarters at Alaejos, and there he made an even bolder alteration 55 to his plans. Captured enemy dispatches included a letter from Berthier to Marshal Soult reporting Napoleon's assessment of the situation: the Emperor could find no English in his front and therefore they must be in full retreat. Napoleon was enjoying excellent health. Details were given of Soult's force, French positions and expected march routes. The opportunity was too good for Sir John Moore to miss: the enemy knew nothing of his whereabouts, while he had full details of theirs. Orders were immediately issued for a change of direction, north-west towards Toro. Moore intended to slash direct at the unsuspecting Soult.

Toro was reached on the evening of 15 December, and union was finally made with Baird at the village of Villalpando late on the 18th. Lord Paget, commanding the 10th and 15th Hussars, made a night march on the 20th/21st and surprised and defeated up to seven hundred French cavalrymen at Sahagún, where Moore now established his headquarters. He was only about twenty-five miles from Soult at Saldaña.

The movement I am making is of the most dangerous kind [he warned Frere]. I not only risk to be surrounded every moment by superior forces, but to have my communication intercepted with the Galicias. I wish it to be apparent to the whole world, as it is to every inhabitant of this army, that we have done everything in our power in support of the Spanish cause, and that we do not abandon it until long after the Spaniards have abandoned us.

For a few more hours the French remained unaware of the danger. Napoleon was resting in Madrid on this 21 December contentedly musing over plans for magnificent alterations to Paris, in celebration of his military glories.

I see from the papers [wrote the Emperor to his Minister of the Interior during the day], that you have laid the foundation-stone of the fountain on the site of the Bastille. I assume that the elephant will stand in the centre of a huge basin filled with water, that it will be a handsome beast, and big enough for people to be able to get inside the howdah on its back . . .

Meanwhile Moore was organising his units into line; deployment was completed on 22 December, the same day that the Cintra Inquiry in London approved the Convention by six votes to one, and thus cleared the smear from Sir Arthur Wellesley's name. Battle against Soult was expected on the 23rd.

But during the 23rd reports came in which were both fearful and pleasing: Soult had realised the true situation after his cavalry had been attacked by Paget and had begun to draw in reinforcements: moreover, French divisions marching south had been suddenly halted, and all available forces in the Madrid area were

Nicolas Soult, Duke of Dalmatia – known to British troops as the Duke of Damnation: Soult later ordered guns to be fired over Moore's grave in honour of his slain adversary.

hurrying north. Napoleon had now realised the unexpected threat to his rear and had reacted violently. At any moment the tiny British army could expect to be surrounded and annihilated.

Clearly, the time had come for the British to pull away – if they could. The luxury of battle with Soult could not be afforded, and each hour became increasingly precious. The mission Moore had set himself had been accomplished: the French had been drawn from the Spaniards. He could do nothing else now; and ahead lay a long dangerous retreat through the mountains. 'At this season of the year,' Moore wrote in his journal, 'in a country without fuel, it is impossible to bivouac; the villages are small, which obliges us to march by corps in succession. Our retreat, therefore, becomes much more difficult.' This proved a masterly understatement. 57

# Chapter 3

# Retreat to Corunna

The retreat to Corunna began on Christmas Eve, 1808. Roads were already crackling with ice, but most of the men failed to realise the threat which now loomed over them, and voiced disappointment over the order to turn away from the promised battle with Soult, Duke of Dalmatia – known to the troops as the 'Duke of Damnation'. Now Moore's first objective was the Esla, and the immediate danger was a junction between Napoleon's and Soult's forces to trap the British before the river could be crossed. Marshal Ney had passed north-west across the Guadarramas on the 21st, with Napoleon following next day – spurring his horse through shoulder-high snowdrifts. Soult had been ordered to strike south-west, and the two main French forces linked on the afternoon of the 27th. But Moore's calculations were just correct: his army had already managed to cross the Esla further west, with Lord Paget's cavalry holding back advance French detachments. Sleet and snow were falling fast; the turgid river was rising in flood and Crauford's brave brigade remained as long as possible to blow up the last bridge. Moore was already at Benevente, where his men emerged sodden and weary through the thick fog.

Both British and French commanders were issuing orders: the first to his army; Napoleon to Joseph back in Madrid. Sir John Moore declared his determination to maintain strict discipline in his army, and to stamp out the grumbling over lack of battle. 'The Commander of the Forces has observed with concern the extreme bad conduct of the troops . . . The misbehaviour of the troops in the column which marched by Valderas to this place exceeds what he could have believed of British soldiers.' These General Orders, dated 27 December, continued: 'It is impossible for the General to explain to his army the motive for the movement he directs . . . When it is proper to fight a battle, he will do it.' Napoleon considered this battle to be imminent, and to his advantage. 'To-day, or tomorrow,' he scribbled to Joseph, 'it is probable that great events will take place. If the English have not already retreated, they are lost; even if they have already moved they shall be pursued to the water's edge, and not half of them shall re-embark.' He added, with exaggeration: 'Put in your newspapers that 36,000 English are surrounded, that I am at Benevente, in their rear, while Soult is in their front.'

Torrents of rain sluiced down upon the soggy plain of Benevente and the river Esla roared in spate – but French cavalry still managed to cross on 29 December. Lord 'Henry' Paget,

*Opposite* The retreat: Moore's army winds up into the harsh mountains towards terrible hardships in the Spanish winter.

one of the most brilliant cavalry officers of the Napoleonic Wars, organised his men to cover the British retreat. A British infantry sergeant described the hectic scene.

The plain was covered with stragglers, and baggage-mules, and followers of the army; the town was filled with tumult; the distant picquets and videttes were seen galloping in from the right and left; the French were pressing forward boldly, and every appearance indicated that the enemy's whole army was come up and passing the river.

Paget ordered his hussars to mount and form under the cover of houses at the edge of the town, then, with considerable coolness, he waited thirty minutes while the main body of French horsemen crossed the river on to the plain. At last Paget ordered the charge. His horses wheeled from behind cover, kicked up the sodden turf, and thundered down upon the French; the enemy fled back to the river and launched their horses through the swirling flood to the far bank. Experienced cavalrymen, they immediately reined their horses back into line and seemed ready to charge again. Six British guns were hastily shoved into position and a barrage landed on the enemy, forcing survivors to retire. Not only had the threat been removed for the moment, but Paget's men had pulled off a considerable *coup*. A captured French officer was escorted to Moore's HQ, blood streaming from his forehead: he introduced himself as General Count Charles Lefèbre-Desnouttes, commander of the cavalry of the Guard and Josephine's thirty-five-year-old nephew. Moore received him with courtesy, washing and binding his wound himself and lending some of his own clothing to replace the general's sodden scarlet, gold, olive and white uniform. A flag of truce was sent across the river to seek the general's baggage; this returned in time for the Count to change for supper.

Retreat continued. But Napoleon's regiments waited two days at Benevente to reorganise; meanwhile Soult fell upon General Romana's Spanish rearguard at Mansilla, causing the rest of the patriot army to flee in panic to Astorga, into which town both Spanish and British forces were crammed on the 30th. Both armies would now have to follow the same retreat road, and the Spaniards were even more deficient in supplies and equipment than their allies. Many of them were already without boots. The situation in Astorga itself was chaotic, with confusion increased by thick fog filtering through the crowded narrow streets. Rioting troops were scattering the contents of houses, and passageways were jammed with baggage wagons, horses, bullock carts, cattle and wailing inhabitants. Fires flared and acrid smoke
60   swirled through the alleys. French advance detachments were

on the outskirts of the town. 'The chatter of the muskets in the distance,' wrote one eye-witness, 'and the monotonous staccato calls of the bugles, mustering the scattered rearguard together, mingled with the cries of the women praying to the Virgin and the uproar created by the cursing of the military . . .' Many troops were made insensible with drink, and when the army pushed on from the town on 1 and 2 January 1809, groaning soldiers lay strewn about the streets in a drunken stupor, easy prey for the first French cavalrymen.

Many had believed Moore would fight a battle at Astorga; he himself had told Romana that this would be the place if he decided to make a stand. But then had come the Spanish rout and the accelerating confusion. Yet Moore's decision to press on fanned the grumbles in his army and led to further deadening demoralisation. Once it became clear that the British would not offer battle, Napoleon decided to quit the scene, leaving for Paris on 2 January. Soult was ordered to continue the pursuit with two divisions of the 8th Corps, plus cavalry, totalling 47,000 men. Many of the units in the British army were fast disintegrating. Morale daily slumped lower. When Bemibre was reached on 2 January men immediately raided the immense wine-vaults and drank themselves unconscious again, and once more many soldiers were too drunk to stagger with the rest of the army. Groups of men and women lay sprawled in the slush, wine dribbling from mouths and nostrils; the French trotted through the grey snow for the slaughter. British commanders struggled to keep discipline in the remainder of the army; only this way would the troops keep together. One commander especially tightened his already taut control: General 'Black Bob' Crauford, feared and respected by his troops. 'You think, because you are Riflemen, you may do whatever you think proper,' he bellowed, 'but I'll teach you the difference before I have done with you.' Two men were caught straying away from his brigade; Crauford immediately ordered a drumhead court-martial which sentenced the culprits to a hundred lashes each. The commander heard another man muttering 'Damn his eyes!' and he too was ordered to be flogged – three hundred lashes. By now darkness had fallen and the weary men moved on, until Crauford halted the column at dawn for sentences to be carried out. 'Although I should obtain the goodwill neither of the officers nor the men of the brigade here by so doing, I am resolved to punish these three men . . . even though the French are at our heels.' The troops were ordered to form a square, into which were marched the three offenders; their comrades stood to

*Overleaf* Men of the 10th Hussars, part of Paget's cavalry rearguard, hold the Esla fords at the start of the retreat to Corunna.

watch the sentence carried out, some of them with 'tears falling down their cheeks from the agony of their bleeding feet, and many were ill with dysentery.' First to be flogged was the man sentenced to three hundred lashes: his Irish wife, watching with the troops, stepped forward to cover his lacerated back when the whipping had finished. Enemy troops were about to attack; the brigade moved on.

On trudged the British troops through the increasing wreckage of retreat: coaches, litters, carts filled with wide-eyed, white-faced wounded. Men and women lost their shoes in the sucking slush; frost-bite became more common.

Our sufferings were so great [wrote one Highlander], that many of the men lost their natural activity and spirits, and became savage in their disposition. The idea of running away, without firing a shot, from the enemy we had beaten so easily at Vimiero, was too galling for their feelings. Each spoke to his fellow, even in common conversation, with bitterness: rage flashed out on the most trifling occasion.

Success at Rolica and Vimiero had ill-conditioned men for setback.

But not all troops lost heart – and amongst those who did, many would have rallied immediately a battle occurred. Although some infantry battalions scattered in search of safety, wine and women, other units and especially the rearguard retained their discipline. And on the afternoon of 3 January this rearguard turned and snapped back at the pursuers. One French general, Colbert in Ney's Corps, became over-confident, and thrust forward with two regiments to force the defile leading to Villafranca. His men advanced with music playing until they reached Cacabelos, six miles south of Villafranca, where the narrow river Cua crossed the road. A squadron of the 15th Light Dragoons was forced to flee over the bridge, taking with them a number of Moore's staff officers. His Military Secretary, Colborne, admitted he had been

in as great a fright as I ever was in my life . . . we had to wheel round, and ride as hard as we could, and expected them on us every minute . . . At last we got to the bridge – covered with Rifles, all jammed upon it. We called out 'Go back! Get into the houses! Get into the houses!'

The Military Secretary reported to Sir John Moore on a nearby hill, and the British commander immediately organised reinforcements for the bridge in the village. A bombardment from the Horse Artillery and rolling musket-fire forced Colbert's men back, but sharp-shooting and volleys continued. British detachments clung to the western bank, to gain retreating time for the rest of the army, but at 4 pm they heard the beat of approaching French drums, and the leading battalions of additional French infantry reached the fighting just before dusk. Colbert crossed the river with his men, and the French began to filter forward. Hand-to-hand fighting broke out in the houses and among the rubble: General Colbert was shot through the head by Rifleman Thomas Plunet of Crauford's 95th and Colbert's *aide-de-camp*, Maubourg, crumpled by his side. Despite the enemy reinforcements, Moore skilfully drew off his troops at 10 pm. The British army pulled back throughout this wild night of the 3rd, along narrow tracks cutting deep into the mountains. Rivers roared at the bottom of the black ravines by the side of the road; men and carts slipped into the chasms; horses' hooves, now unshod, gushed with blood; the wind howled and the sleet hissed down. The French were often only a few hundred yards behind and further skirmishing broke out at Nogales on the 4th. Food was almost non-existent; men sucked strips of leather to find nourishment. The sullen hills echoed with cracking pistol shots as horses were slaughtered – Lord Paget had ordered mounts to be destroyed as soon as they were unable to keep up, and when no noise was permitted the animals had to be dispatched with knives or hammer blows. The sight of a tough cavalryman kneeling and weeping by his favourite horse became painfully common.

The countryside grew even more desolate on 5 January as the army crossed the high harsh ranges of Galicia. Stabbing blasts of wind knocked men from their feet; they crawled instead. A veteran soldier of the 71st Foot found the body of a young woman, frozen to death, with a whimpering baby still clinging to the mother's icy white neck.

One of General Moore's staff officers came up and desired the infant to be brought to him. He rolled it in his cloak, amidst the blessing of every spectator. Never shall I efface the benevolence of his look when he said, 'Unfortunate infant, you shall be my future care.'

A soldier's wife of the 92nd took up another baby, born a few moments before his mother had died in a bloody snow-drift. An astonishing number of women were still surviving, feet and legs bare and running red, stumbling and crawling and often dragging half-dead children with them. A German commissary officer, Schaumann, described the scene on the 5th:

Every minute a horse would collapse beneath its rider, and be shot dead. The road was strewn with dead horses, bloodstained snow, broken carts, scrapped ammunition, boxes, cases, spiked guns, dead mules, donkeys and dogs, starved and frozen soldiers, women and children . . . The road frequently followed a zigzag course along the very edge of a precipice . . . We waded through snow and mud over the bodies of dead men and horses. The howling wind, as it whistled past the ledges of rock and through the bare trees, sounded to the ear like the groaning of the damned.

The fifty miles from Villafranca to Lugo, reached on 6 January, were the most hellish of the whole retreat. But now came the prospect of battle. Stores had been brought up from Corunna; reports indicated the enemy to be suffering as much as with the British. Soult advanced to the British positions late on the 6th with a powerful force of cavalry and infantry, and early on the 7th a French battery opened up against the British centre. Moore halted his army and prepared to fight. But Soult now knew he had Moore's main force in front of him, rather than the rearguard alone, and he only permitted cautious probing throughout the day. A feint against the British left was attempted at dusk, but Moore rapidly rallied his men and repulsed the enemy. As expected, the smell of battle had brought British stragglers scurrying back into the ranks, and heads were lifted and arms found new strength. Soult still held back from outright attack on 8 January; Moore, while willing to accept defensive battle, refused to move his men forward against the French. Soult declined to take up the challenge and Moore ordered the retreat to continue. Men moved out at 10 pm on the 8th in drenching, freezing rain, leaving bright bivouac fires to deceive the French. Grumbling broke out almost immediately. Why, asked many soldiers, did the retreat continue? 'The Duke of Damnation' should have been chased and mauled; they should have been allowed to do some hacking down, instead of suffering it from the French. Moore knew better, and so did one wise sergeant in his army who wrote: 'This was a season of singular and almost unexampled peril.' The British army, explained this veteran in his memoirs:

was not in a condition to fight more than one battle. It was unprovided with draught cattle, had no means of transporting reserve ammunition, no magazines, no hospitals, no second line, no provisions . . . The state of the magazines decided the matter; for there was not bread for another day's consumption in the stores at Lugo.

Moore had dispatched orders to Admiral Hood from Villafranca on the 3rd, and again from Lugo on the 7th: transport vessels must be brought to Corunna to take off the troops. Now, on the 9th, he could only hope the vessels would arrive in time, and meanwhile had to stimulate remaining strength in his staggering army. Food was again short, although some salt fish and rum rations were distributed at Quitterez on the 9th – with unfortunate effect.

As we had neither fires nor kettles [wrote the commissary officer, August Schaumann], the salt fish was eagerly swallowed raw, while the rum . . .

Shoeless in the snow, men of the British rearguard try to beat back the probing French.

was poured down afterwards. The combination of the two in empty stomachs resulted in the death of many of the men on the spot, while several others went mad.

One berserk soldier stood swaying in the middle of the road, bayonet fixed, shouting he was General Moore: he ordered the army to halt, turn and give battle, and the first man who dared try pass would be killed. Troopers rode over him and left his mangled body in the mud.

On 10 January the first units entered Betzanos. Between five and six thousand men had fallen in the retreat so far: the march

A meeting of English
officers during the
Peninsula campaign.
*From a satirical sketch by
Carle Vernet.*

from Lugo to this point had cost the army double the men who had
fallen in all preceding stages. But now only twelve miles remained
and these through pleasant, undulating countryside; behind
reared the black, dripping mountains, all around lay fields of
rye and orchards of orange trees. The sea was a day's march away.
The advance troops reached Corunna on the 11th and eagerly
looked for the rescue fleet. An empty harbour confronted them. The
vessels had been delayed by contrary winds at Vigo, and although
one or two transports arrived during the afternoon, the bulk of the
army remained stranded with their backs to the sea and the French
in front. Hot food, new shoes, weapons and ammunition were
hastily distributed as unit after unit wound into the shadowy streets
during the night of the 11th. Almost immediately, and throughout
the 12th, regiments were deployed in defensive positions.

Above the port loomed two hill ranges. The first, Monte Mero,
was slightly lower than the other, Peñasquedo. Moore had insufficient men to occupy both features, but deployed troops along

the Monte Mero where the hillsides, strewn with boulders and scrub, offered excellent defensive positions. This would provide the British army's right flank, while the centre would be based on the village of Elviña about three miles from Corunna and situated on a low saddle connecting the two hill ranges. The left flank extended to the impassable estuary of the Mero. Corunna therefore offered excellent opportunities for blocking the French, except for a weak section of the line on the far right where the hill ranges softened into open countryside. Moore attempted to cover the weakness by deploying as many men as possible on the right – as much as half his total strength.

The bulk of the naval transports arrived during the next thirty-six hours and initial embarkation began – the sick, dismounted cavalrymen, the best of the surviving horses, and fifty-two guns. Moore intended to fight the approaching battle without cavalry, and without artillery except for eight British and four Spanish guns. Other preparations were made: during the night of the 12th and early on the 13th massive explosions rent the heavy air and shattered windows – the bridge over the Mero had been blown, plus a huge reserve of explosive powder sent by the British to help the Spaniards and stored just outside the town. Inside Corunna itself the streets were clogged with departing men and bundles of stores; horses were being dragged unwillingly on to the boats – other horses, less fit but equally favoured by their riders, were being slaughtered or turned loose. One cavalryman unsaddled his mount for the last time, sent him away and boarded his boat, only to find his horse plunging into the water behind him. Twice the animal swam like a dog to the transport vessel, but could not be taken on board. 'All those who witnessed this incident had tears in their eyes,' wrote Schaumann.

Sir John Moore, seemingly inexhaustible, rode from one defensive position to another, encouraging his men, issuing orders, making final preparations for the imminent attack. He had already written his last dispatch for Lord Castlereagh; this dwelt upon the events of the last few weeks – the unwillingness of the Spaniards to fight when he had been at Salamanca; his diversion to the north against Soult; the inevitable retreat. The report made sad reading.

I would not have believed, had I not witnessed it, that a British army could, in so short a time, have been so completely disorganised. Its conduct during the late marches has been infamous, beyond belief. I can say nothing in its favour except that when there was a prospect of fighting the Enemy, the men were then orderly, and seemed pleased and determined to do their duty.

Now the prospect of fighting had returned and with it the chance of redemption. But the chill dawn of 16 January brought no sign of enemy activity; Sir John Moore stayed in the front lines until 10 am, then rode back to Corunna leaving instructions for three guns to be fired if the enemy appeared about to move forward. Back in the town Moore gave instructions for the final retirement of the main army to the hundred transports now riding the swell in the bay: this last withdrawal would take place in the night. Moore and his staff had an early lunch, then walked down to the harbour to supervise embarkation. Orderlies began to pack the documents and belongings in the headquarters. Just before 2 pm Moore mounted to ride back to the lines along the Monte Mero: he was about to put spurs to his horse when three guns boomed from the hills. Battle had begun.

Moore and his staff galloped through units which had already been turned from their march to the harbour and were now heading back for the battle. Up in the lines, increasing activity could be observed in the French positions. British troops lined their defences; men murmured, checked their weapons, or watched the bustling French in silence. Both armies were of equal manpower strength – about 15,000 – but the French had more artillery. Now three enemy columns began to advance, the noise of the rattling drums was suddenly obliterated by the roars from supporting guns: one column pushed towards the left, another towards the centre, and the third – initially with the most impact – towards the British right. Moore had expected the latter and felt confident that the additional strength which he had placed in this sector would deal with the threat. Lord Paget was ordered to counter-advance when a suitable opportunity occurred. Meanwhile Moore galloped towards the firing in the centre: he judged correctly that Elviña village would be the point of fiercest fighting and the place where he would be most needed.

A swarm of French ran down the hillside towards the village. British defenders could hear shrill enemy voices – '*En avant! En Avant! Tué! Tué! Tué!*' Bullets suddenly hummed and hissed among the stone walls, ricocheting among the rocks, thudding into the wood and turf. Advance picquets were driven back. The French pressed on and their cannon blasted smoking holes into the defensive positions. One house fell, then another. For a while it seemed the British line would come tumbling back. 'All were anxious for the appearance of Sir John Moore,' wrote Charles Napier. 'There was a feeling that, under him we could not be beaten. . . "Where is the General?" was now heard along that

The burial of Sir John Moore at Corunna. This painting typifies the romanticism surrounding Moore's death: he not buried in the dark of night, but early in the morning. *From the painting by G. Jones*

General Don Joseph Palafox, vain and ostentatious, won glory through his defence of Saragossa in the spring 1809, when he returned from military retirement to command outnumbered forces in the besieged city. The siege lasted 61 days; the enemy retreated, only to return with vastly superior strength. Palafox was taken as a prisoner to France.
*From the painting by Goya*

part of the line.' The general appeared, with lathered horse rearing and throwing up the dirt, and a massive cheer ran along the ranks. Reinforcements were thrown into the village, streets were regained, then lost again. Ground near Moore became churned by French artillery bombardments; one shell narrowly missed the general, and he was still controlling his shying horse when another shot ripped off the leg of a nearby soldier, who rolled in the mud clawing at his wound with terrible screams. 'This is nothing, my lads,' shouted Moore amidst the thunder. 'Keep your ranks. Take that man away. My good fellow, don't make such a noise; we must bear these things better.' The British line steadied, and held. One regiment, the 4th, was in danger of being encircled: Moore ordered a preventive manoeuvre and shouted his satisfaction at the manner in which this was accomplished. 'That is exactly how it should be done.' Troops already in the naval transports crowded the gunwales to see the battle on the slopes above them: thin lines of men, blue and red, running and advancing and criss-crossing

Sir John Moore gallops up to the Battle of Corunna to direct the British defence; moments later the British commander falls mortally wounded through the swirling smoke; guns belching thick smoke and the echoes sounding round the harbour; bugles shrilly blaring. The French struck at Elviña again and clung fast to bloody ground gained, attempting to deploy for a further advance. Moore seemed to be everywhere and always in the nick of time. The 50th and 42nd regiments were hurled against the French and drove them back through the village. Then disaster almost occurred: the 42nd, believing they were being relieved, started to pull back. Once again Moore appeared in exactly the right position, calm and precise. 'My brave 42nd, join your comrades.' Back they went. At the same time General Paget obeyed his previous order to strike at the opportune moment; he had carefully chosen his time, and now he advanced with the Reserve. The French began to give ground, back through the cloying smoke.

But British losses were increasing. General Baird, second-in-command of the army, had just left the battlefield supported in his blood-wet saddle and with his right arm mangled by grapeshot. And now General Sir John Moore was suddenly flung from his shrieking horse. He lay on his side for a moment, then struggled to raise himself and his aides believed him unhurt – and then they saw the mess suddenly spurting through the uniform on his left breast and shoulder. Officers laid him against a bank. He made no sound, but continued to watch the battle in progress to the front of him: the 42nd regiment was advancing; he gave a tight smile. His uniform was stripped from his chest to reveal the ghastly wound, and a medical officer took one look and muttered 'hopeless'. Moore's shoulder had been shattered, with a thick piece of uniform driven deep into the gaping wound still with two buttons attached; his left arm remained attached by only thin strips of skin, his ribs were smashed and stuck out at all angles, and his chest muscles had been torn into long strips, which had then knotted together with the force of the blow. Sir John Moore surveyed the battle for a few moments longer and was then lifted on to a blanket. His sword hilt rose up and jabbed into his open wound, and an aide started to unbuckle the belt: Moore told him to leave it be. 'I had rather it should go out of the field with me.'

The British advance continued under the command of Sir John Hope while Moore was carried back down into Corunna. Schaumann witnessed the scene.

Among many wounded men who were borne past us into the town there appeared at about 4 o'clock a party of several *aides-de-camp* and officers, marching very slowly and sadly behind six soldiers bearing a wounded man in a blood-stained blanket slung upon two poles.

The general was carried carefully into a darkened headquarters room, now deserted, all belongings having already been taken on board. Moore uttered no moans or complaints except to murmur: 'I fear I shall be a long time in dying . . . It is a great uneasiness . . . It is great pain.' He also whispered: 'I have always wished to die this way.' Each time someone came into the room he turned his marble face towards them and asked: 'Are the French beat?' Hearing the reply he closed his glazing eyes and said: 'I hope the people of England will be satisfied.' Sir John Moore died at about eight o'clock, just before the first British troops began to march back through the town from the battle to the waiting warships.

Fighting had died down in the evening. Sir John Hope reckoned a successful embarkation to be more important than a pursuit of the French. Both sides were exhausted, but the British departure could now take place unmolested, although speed was still essential. Both French and British had probably lost about the same number of men, between 700 and 900. Throughout the night the exhausted soldiers moved through Corunna, still in good order but with uniforms in tatters, covered with blood and filth and with gaunt, hollow-eyed faces. Citizens in the streets made the sign of the cross as the soldiers passed through the flickering patches of lamp-light, because they looked so terrible.

A few detachments of French troops moved cautiously forward during the early hours of 17 January; at 8 am one or two guns opened fire upon the town and the fleet. Shortly after, Sir John Moore was buried near the landward bastion of Corunna citadel. Time and means were too short for a coffin to be prepared, and the long body was merely wrapped in the general's dirty military cloak. The fleet sailed during the day, harassed by French artillery-fire which sank one transport and drove others aground. Men were safely transferred to other vessels in the best Royal Navy tradition, and the British army began its five-day voyage back to England – and back to fierce political controversy over the ill-fated expedition into Spain and over future plans for the Peninsula. Moore's opinions on the latter subject were made plain in his last dispatch to Castlereagh.

If I succeed in embarking the Army, I shall send it to England. It is quite unfit for further service until it has been refitted, which can best be done there; and I cannot think, after what has happened, that there can be any intention of sending a British force again into Spain.

But amongst the weary troops on the overcrowded, stinking transports were many who shared another thought – 'We shall return.'

# Chapter 4

# Return

**R**oyal Navy vessels disembarked the remains of the Peninsular army in English ports between 18 and 25 June. Many of the men were landed at night to avoid alarming local inhabitants by their fearful appearance. Regiments were scattered between one ship and another, equipment had been left behind, some units would have to be rebuilt from nothing. Clearly, weeks would be required for necessary re-organisation and recovery. This at least allowed improvement to be introduced, including lessons learnt from the Spanish campaign, even down to minor details of uniform and equipment: brown leather belts and harnesses were substituted for black, which had been found harder to keep clean and quicker to rot; more mares were introduced into the cavalry, rather than the previous rigid preference for stallions. Veterans of the Spanish fighting handed their experience to newcomers; Crauford's units were soon to become the famous Light Division, still subject to his harsh demands; equipment was re-issued; new weapons produced. On 1 February a General Order was issued from the War Office:

The benefits derived to an army from the example of a distinguished Commander do not terminate at his death; his virtues live in the recollections of his associates, and his fame remains the strongest incentive to great and glorious action.

But where would these 'great and glorious' events take place? And who would be the new commander?

Mr George Ponsonby rose in the House of Commons on 24 February 1809, to demand an inquiry into the campaign in Spain. His motion was defeated, but only after vigorous debate. Many MPs agreed with a remark made by Mr Whitbread in the House on 31 January: had Sir Arthur Wellesley been in Spain, the affair would have ended differently. But in the debate on 24 February, Foreign Secretary Canning gave an indication of official thinking:

*Opposite* William Carr Beresford, portly, competent, a close friend of Wellesley, who took over command of the Portuguese forces in early 1809.

If we have been obliged to quit Spain, we have left it with fresh laurels blooming on our brows . . . Whatever may be the fruits of Bonaparte's victories in other respects, the spirit of the Spanish nation is yet unsubdued.

Yet how long would the Peninsula remain unsubdued without further British help? The Spaniards had only just been thrown from the city of Saragossa after the fortress had been besieged since 20 December, brilliantly defended by the dashing General Palafox

77

and subject to repeated French attacks directed first by Moncey, then Mortier, Junot and finally Lannes. The fall of Saragossa set free 25,000 French soldiers, and the threat to Portugal loomed large. Sir John Craddock was now in command at Lisbon with barely 10,000 men. Relations with the Portuguese were deplorable, and although Craddock attempted to strengthen defences, it seemed certain evacuation would be necessary. Sir John Moore himself had declared the country could not be held.

Sir Arthur Wellesley disagreed. Admiring Moore as a man and a soldier, and rigorously opposing those who now criticised him, he nevertheless took the reverse view with regard to the Peninsula. 'I have always been of the opinion,' wrote Wellesley to Castlereagh in a memorandum dated 7 March, 'that Portugal might be defended whatever might be the result of the contest in Spain.' But he took care to stipulate that defence must involve the dispatch of at least 20,000 British troops, including 4,000 cavalry; the Portuguese army must be reorganised; Spain should be encouraged to pin down French troops through guerrilla warfare. The Portuguese approached Wellesley with an offer of supreme command of their forces; Wellesley, with more ambitious ideas in mind, declined, and General William Beresford – a personal friend – was appointed. Hopes of an early decision over Spain received a setback on 17 March when the Duke of York was obliged to resign as Commander-in-Chief of the British Army: the Duke's mistress, Mary Ann Clarke, was accused of using her position to sell commissions and promotions. York's successor at the Horse Guards was Sir David Dundas, old, cautious and dilatory. At the same time, Wellesley's influential 7 March memorandum had had a powerful effect on Lord Castlereagh and, after a heated Cabinet discussion in mid-March, Wellesley was informed of his hoped-for command, officially dated 6 April 1809. He was to proceed to the Peninsula as Beresford's superior: his orders were to throw back the French. Instructions laid down firm priority, perhaps a lesson from the vague and mistaken instructions which had sent Moore into Spain too late in the year and with insufficient strength: 'The defence of Portugal you will consider as the first and most immediate object of your attention.' Spanish operations must wait and would have to receive the firm sanction of the British Cabinet.

Napoleon had also been issuing firm orders: remaining British military presence in the Peninsula must be driven into the sea. At the end of March, Soult pushed forward into Portugal from the north, over the Minho river, with Oporto his target; in the centre,

Marshal Victor moved against Spanish forces under Cuesta; Sebastiani drove against La Mancha. Cuesta's troops were scattered at Medellin on 28 March, with the Spanish general being ridden down by his own cavalry and having to be dragged clear, bruised and nearly senseless, before the French swept the field. Seventy miles to the east La Mancha's forces were heavily defeated at Ciudad Real. Soult took and sacked Oporto on the 29th. French forces were converging on Lisbon from the north and west. Soult had about 20,000 men under his command; Ney, in Galicia, had as many more and Victor, now at Merida, had an even larger force. British strength would total about 22,000 men, with the support of about 10,000 Portuguese.

Sir Arthur Wellesley reached Lisbon on 22 April. The capital was strewn with flowers and banners in his honour, but the gilt hardly covered the grime of war. Within forty-eight hours, despite interfering ceremonies to celebrate his arrival, Wellesley had completed his plans: first he would thrust north, defeat Soult and re-take Oporto; this accomplished, he would dash south again before Victor could strike into Portugal. Victor would be defeated if possible in cooperation with the Spanish under Cuesta, and    79

Wellesley would then stab into Spain via Merida and drive for
Madrid. Wellesley joined his troops at Coimbra on 2 May. Speed
and sureness were the two necessities, and he had to spend seven
precious days organising his army: the commissariat system was
improved, to avoid the dangers of supplies failing in the intricate
manoeuvring; baggage was reduced to a minimum; the infantry
was divided into divisions for easier command and logistical
support; units were organised so that one Portuguese infantry
battalion was placed in each of the five British brigades; every
brigade was given a permanent company of riflemen to strengthen
the skirmishing role. Wellesley then split his forces into three in an
attempt to deal with the multiple threats facing him. General
William Beresford, ambitious, newly promoted, and with a liking
for riding about Lisbon with much pomp and many attendants,
was given command of 1,875 British troops and 4,200 Portuguese,
with orders to block any move by Soult from northern Portugal
eastwards towards Victor. Secondly, General Mackenzie was
ordered to prepare to stop Victor himself with 4,500 British and
7,500 Portuguese troops. This left Wellesley with 16,000 British
and 2,400 newly-recruited Portuguese for his advance up the main
route from Coimbra to Oporto against Soult, although recent

intelligence indicated Soult would probably outnumber him by 5,000 troops – all of them veterans. With this sombre thought Wellesley began his march on 8 May, having given Beresford forty-eight hours' start to allow him to push further east.

British and Portuguese forces advanced north in the strong May sunshine. Maximum speed was maintained throughout the 8th and 9th and within twenty-four hours contact had been made with enemy outposts on the Vouga river south of Oporto. These forces hastily withdrew before the approaching British, moving back into the city to avoid an outflanking movement by Wellesley.

I must note the beautiful effect of our engagement [wrote one participant, Colonel Hawker]. It commenced about sunrise on one of the finest spring mornings possible, on an immense tract of heath, with a pine wood in rear of the enemy. So little was the slaughter, and so regular the manoeuvring, that it all appeared more like a sham fight on Wimbledon Common.

Despite increasing weariness the Allied troops were hurried on-wards during the 10th and 11th and another outflanking move-ment was attempted almost within the city suburbs, but the French pulled back again. During the night of 11 May the enemy retired over the river Douro, which flows wide through a deep gorge in Oporto itself, and at 2 am on the 12th the remaining bridge exploded with an echoing roar. Soult on the far bank had ordered all boats to be destroyed; the river was believed impassable; he thought the only remaining British threat would be from the sea. Soult therefore seemed safe until British warships were moved north to make the sea-borne attack.

Yet Wellesley also felt temporarily satisfied. He had forced back a stronger French army with a loss of only 150 men to the enemy's 300 and his new Portuguese troops had performed well; above all, Beresford was carrying out his orders in superb fashion and had reached Lamego on the 10th. Communications between Soult and Victor were severed, and contact had been made with local Portuguese forces under General Silviera. And with this excellent progress now came an added spice of extreme good luck. Wellesley was standing with a telescope to his eye in a shady convent on a hillside in the Vila Nova suburb: he could see enemy activity on the far side of the river, with the bulk of the French force apparently concentrated westwards towards the sea; eastwards were few patrols or picquets, and the steep slopes would prevent enemy observation if a crossing could be made in this area. If a crossing could be made . . . And precisely at this moment, invaluable information was hurried to the British commander. A ferry four miles upstream could be repaired and be in service by

Troops under Sir John
Murray slip across the
Douro upstream from
Oporto to block the
French escape.

noon. Further, a local barber had slipped over by small boat to say the enemy had overlooked four wine barges under the cliffs on the French side of the river. Volunteers were immediately sent to collect these craft; within an hour the ripples of their wakes had spread undetected across the broad sunlit river and they lay hidden on the British bank. Wellesley was informed. 'Well, let the men cross,' came his casual reply. The redcoats began to trickle over the blue-grey water in anxious groups of thirty.

Soult lay enjoying an early siesta and his men were apparently also preoccupied; but each minute dragged. At noon Wellesley scribbled a message for Beresford: 'My advance guards are crossing in Boats . . . the passage goes but slowly.' Sir John Murray was ordered to cross by the ferry further upstream. British troops were now clambering up the steep slopes and slipping into the shadowy alley-ways, and soon they must surely be seen. Buildings were hastily fortified for the expected French counter-attack. Incredibly, this remained unlaunched for an hour, one possible reason being Soult's mistake in believing the red coats were worn by his own Swiss mercenaries. At last, *tirailleurs* ran shouting and firing towards the new British positions supported by three infantry battalions, and the silence above Oporto was split by heavy, incessant musket volleys. French artillery was dragged forward – fire from British howitzers on the far side of the river immediately shattered the first French weapon. The enemy attack failed; more British troops flooded across; a second attack was repulsed, and the French began to evacuate nearby streets. Sentries fled from the boats and almost immediately Portuguese civilians darted forward to row them across to the cheering British. The Brigade of Guards entered the fight, then the 29th, to strike a third French counter-attack in the flank. French troops began to stream from the city and Soult left half his magnificent lunch untouched – Wellesley enjoyed it for his tea. Only 123 Allied troops had been lost, compared with 300 enemy killed and wounded plus 70 guns captured and 1,500 men abandoned in Oporto hospital. The rest of the Allied army, the guns and the baggage, were brought over during the remainder of 12 May while the men received a rapturous and wine-flowing welcome from the liberated Portuguese. Early next morning the chase began.

On the same day Vienna fell to Napoleon; the Emperor's elation over this brilliant victory against the Austrians was soon to be dampened by the latest news of this near-disaster in the Peninsula. Soult barely managed to avoid total defeat. His routed army retreated towards Amarante, passing across the front of troops sent over the Douro by Wellesley under the command of Sir John Murray; but the British force lacked strength through inefficient deployment and the opportunity was thrown away. The next five days were hellish, for both the French and the Allies. Black thunder-clouds massed on the 13th and torrential rain turned tracks into quagmires as Soult slipped into the sodden mountains; gentle streams became roaring floods within minutes, and bridges, roads, men and horses were swept away. The shivering, exhausted British troops stumbled over the swollen carcasses of animals and humans, and enemy wounded were left behind together with an increasing amount of valuable equipment. Portuguese partisans plunged into the French to torture stragglers; Soult's men reacted by hanging civilians and razing houses. 'The route of their column on their retreat,' reported Wellesley, 'could be traced by the smoke of the villages to which they had set fire.'

Beresford used his own initiative with excellent results: a French force under Loison had been beaten back by Portuguese under Silviera east of Lamego on the 10th and had pulled away towards Guimaraes. Not until the morning of the 15th did Beresford hear of Oporto's liberation and Soult's retreat, but he had already decided to let Loison go, and to head north for Chaves under his original orders to prevent Soult moving east towards Victor. His troops were on the move from Lamego when he received instructions from Wellesley to undertake this precise march. Soult managed to unite with Loison, but the French were on a single road, both ends of which – Braga and Chaves – might soon be in Allied hands. Only one escape route remained – the branch track from near Salamonde running to Montalegre and Orense. Silviera had already been ordered by Beresford to march across country to Salamonde from Amarante, and, late on the 15th, he should have almost reached this vital junction.

Conditions were still appalling. Mud layered the roads in a clinging black scum; swirling mist and thick storm clouds covered the rugged terrain. But Soult managed to reach Salamonde first, and only one obstacle remained – the passage over the river Cavado, now in angry spate. The five-mile-long French column found itself hemmed in by mountains on either side, by local Portuguese militia on the far bank of the Cavado and by Wellesley's force pressing close behind. Brave French volunteers forced their way on to the half-destroyed bridge and established a hold on the other bank. Grim fighting took place in the pouring rain throughout the night of 15 May as the French tried desperately to repair the bridge for the main army. Gradually they crossed, leaving the river almost dammed by dead bodies. Soult pushed on during the 16th and 17th, with units able to move faster now that baggage and equipment had been abandoned. Contact was still maintained between the opposing armies; Wellesley reached Montalegre on the 18th and slept in the cottage used by Soult for a few snatched hours of rest the previous night. But already the French were fleeing over the border into Spain. British troops were dropping from weariness and lack of food; many were without shoes, lost in the mud and floods. Even before the Oporto battle men had marched 120 miles in six days. And Sir Arthur Wellesley had achieved the first of his objectives: the recapture of Oporto. Soult had lost 4,000 men and masses of equipment. Wellesley, who had suffered only 300 killed and wounded with an additional 200 stragglers and sick, had now to turn south again to face Victor, who, according to a report from General Mackenzie, had crossed the border in full force. On 18 May the pursuit was abandoned. The Allied army was allowed to move back in easy stages while Wellesley rode ahead, reaching Oporto again on 22 May; he learnt, with some relief, that Mackenzie's assessment had been alarmist – Victor had thrown forward a strong reconnaissance but had now retired.

Wellesley took time in which to reorganise his men near
84  Abrantes. Apart from the state of his troops a further Allied

campaign would anyway have been complicated by Wellesley's
lack of money with which to pay for stores and equipment.
Moreover, despite recent successes, the British commander apparently believed improvements were urgently needed in his army:
letters home soon sounded even peevish when describing his men,
with his ill-humour probably increased by the lukewarm reception
given in London to news of Soult's headlong retreat. 'The army
behave terribly ill,' complained Wellesley to Castlereagh on the
last day of May. 'They are a rabble who cannot bear success any
more than Sir John Moore's army could bear failure. I am
endeavouring to tame them.' And again on 17 June: 'We are an
excellent army on parade, an excellent one to fight; but we are
worse than an enemy in a country . . . either defeat or success

would dissolve us.' Wellesley's chief complaint stemmed from the practice of plundering – a sure sign of lack of discipline. Yet the thieving also indicated restlessness; the troops were soon bored and this in turn underlined the resilience of the army. Hardships suffered in Soult's pursuit were soon forgotten and the troops were anxious to flex their muscles again. Dull training and musket practice seemed a poor substitute for inflicting defeat on 'Boney's' much vaunted warriors. And Wellesley himself shared similar restlessness. As early as 22 May he had suggested to the Spanish General Cuesta that combined operations should be undertaken against Victor, but Cuesta seemed slow to respond. Even if rapid agreement had been forthcoming, Wellesley would still have been hamstrung through lack of finance; he wrote to the British Ambassador in Lisbon, Villiers, on 11 June: 'I should begin immediately but I cannot venture to stir without money.' By 25 June Wellesley had managed to obtain over £100,000; his army marched forty-eight hours later and crossed into Spain on 4 July, on the same day that Napoleon slipped across the Danube to smash the Austrian army at the Battle of Wagram and thus underline his supremacy in northern Europe. Apart from a few minor rebellions the Peninsula now marked the only area of active opposition to Bonaparte's military might.

Wellesley's army, divided into two main columns, entered Plasencia on 8 and 9 July, and next day the British commander rode on with his staff to Almarez on the Tagus for his first meeting with the Spanish military leader, Gregorio Cuesta. The interview promised to be stormy. Spanish pledges of food and transport for British units when they crossed the border had been broken; the Spaniards had seemed reluctant to agree to ambitious plans for a joint operation – and now Victor had been able to pull back to Talavera, seventy miles south-west of Madrid, where he would be in contact with the main French force in Spain. To add to the general gloom, Wellesley arrived five hours late for the Almarez meeting, having been led by a useless guide. Cuesta, aged over seventy, had still to recover from his narrow escape at Medellin: he had to be carried in a coach while campaigning, drawn by nine mules, and he appeared to be easily exhausted. Further complications arose from his inability to speak French or English, and from his suspicions that the British minister, Frere, plotted with the Central Junta against him. Nevertheless, a four-hour discussion in the lamp-lit HQ resulted in some kind of agreement – mainly because Cuesta feared Wellesley might withdraw back to Portugal if a plan were not agreed upon. And proud Cuesta, despite his military deficiencies, age and physical handicaps, remained as anxious as Wellesley to thrash the French. Together they could outnumber the enemy, although Wellesley had serious doubts over the reliability of the Spanish regular forces. Victor had over 20,000 men at Talavera; Sebastiani had a further 22,000 at Madridejos, seventy-five miles south-east of the capital. Stationed in Madrid itself were 12,000 troops. All were theoretically under the command of King Joseph Bonaparte, who had Marshal Jourdan as his Chief of Staff. The three forces could be concentrated within forty-eight hours if Toledo were selected as the junction point; this would give a total of 50,000 French veterans against 35,000 Spanish and 20,000 British and Portuguese. Wellesley wisely decided such enemy concentration must be avoided at all costs, despite the dangers of being encircled if the three forces remained separate. Another Spanish force, totalling 30,000 men and commanded by General Venegas, was deployed in mountains south of Sebastiani's contingent and could therefore exert pressure from this direction; meanwhile Cuesta and Wellesley would join forces at Oropesa, thirty miles west of Talavera, on 21 July. Both would then strike at Victor while Venegas moved north on the 16th towards Madrid, via Aranjuez. A small Allied force, consisting of British, Spanish and Portuguese troops under Sir Robert Wilson, would advance east along the Tietar valley, north of, but parallel to, the Tagus: this would hinder any surprise attack by troops under Soult, Ney or Mortier from the north, and would also impose an additional threat on the French in Madrid.

Wellesley's units press
hard against the French
rearguard in the rugged
terrain around Salam-
onde as Soult flees into
Spain.

All looked excellent on paper, and to start with events moved
according to plan. Wellesley ordered the British army to advance on
the 17th, and his regiments crossed the Tietar next day. Junction
with the Spanish forces took place as arranged on the 21st; within a
few hours both armies had left Oropesa and were moving along
parallel paths towards Victor at Talavera. Spanish cavalry clashed
with French dragoons and horse artillery at noon on the 22nd, but
as soon as Victor realised the presence of British troops he ordered
hasty retreat three miles back to the Alberche. Although the French
general had previously placed infantry and artillery in defensive
positions behind this river, his situation remained precarious; he
had only 22,000 men with which to withstand an offensive by
55,000. Cuesta agreed to an attack to start at dawn next day,
23 July.

Wellesley accordingly rose soon after 2 am on the 23rd. The
British army was positioned north of the Alberche before the first
traces of daylight, under thick olive and cork tree cover. Grey
dawn swept over the troops. Orders were ready to send regiments
thrusting upon the French from the north as soon as Cuesta opened
the attack by a drive from the main Talavera–Madrid road. Men
stood waiting in a silence broken only by the jingle of cavalry

88

harness, the occasional stamp of hooves and the scrape of a bayonet. The sun rose, and men began to murmur in impatience. Cuesta had still to make his move. Wellesley rolled himself in his military cloak and fell asleep. The Spanish attack remained unlaunched at 6 am and even Sir Arthur Wellesley could stand the wait no longer. He cantered over to Cuesta's camp to find the old general slumped upon plump pillows: his army was too exhausted, he explained, and insufficient preparations had been made. Tomorrow they would attack. Wellesley rode back to his troops in disgust and ordered his regiments to stand down.

Victor made good use of this timely breathing-space and withdrew his army soon after nightfall on the 23rd. British scouts reported other French troops moving to join Victor's forces and Wellesley refused the now-eager Cuesta's demand for foolish pursuit. The British general gave vent to his anger in a letter to Frere on the 24th.

Although my troops have been on forced marches, engaged in operations with the enemy, the success of which I must say depended upon them, they have had nothing to eat, while the Spanish army have had plenty . . . I can only say, that I have never seen an army so ill-treated in any country, or, considering that all depends upon its operations, one which deserved good treatment so much.

Anglo-Spanish relations were now deplorable: British reports that treachery on Cuesta's staff had led to Victor's withdrawal late on the 23rd were met with Spanish allegations that Wellesley himself had not wanted to attack, and had used Cuesta to cloak his own reluctance. One factor remained indisputable: a unique opportunity had been missed. And, on 24 July, it seemed another chance would be long in coming. The Spanish army under Venegas had failed to fulfil its blocking role, and Sebastiani was allowed to reinforce Victor despite a mad pursuit of the French undertaken by Cuesta's scattered forces on the 24th and early 25th. Fortunately Victor did not seize this occasion to turn back upon the unsupported British; by noon on the 25th Cuesta's energy had evaporated and he pulled back his troops to join Wellesley again. Sooner than expected, the French were approaching for battle. Wellesley, who within a few hours was to earn himself the title of Viscount Wellington of Talavera, had to suffer the indignity of going down upon his knees before the aged Spanish general, to beg him to move back into stronger positions by Talavera itself. His request was graciously granted; Spanish and British regiments moved back and swung into line. Early on 27 July 1809, British, French and Spanish troops prepared for imminent, large-scale battle.

# Chapter 5

# Talavera to Torres

By the afternoon of the 27th an enemy attack had still to be launched. Some men began to hope it would remain delayed until the morrow; others wanted it over with. They stood in line under the broiling sun, or crouched in the small shade afforded by packs stretched across musket props. Flies buzzed about them; veterans gave their weapons a last clean and wipe and smoked their pipes; recruits sweated and shivered. Before them, across Portina stream, stretched the dusty Talavera plain ringed to the south by red rocks and to the north by shimmering blue mountains. Vultures wheeled in expectation.

The shallow Portina marked the front of the Allied position, running down from the mountains in the north to the walls of Talavera town on the bank of the Tagus. Cuesta's main Spanish force filled the right of the line, extending from Talavera to a central redoubt named Pajar; British troops continued the line from this redoubt to the lozenge-shaped Medellin hill, just to the west of the Portina and opposite another ridge, Cascajal, which was to be left to the French. The weakest part of the line, defended by a few Spanish units and covered by British cavalry, existed between Medellin hill and the north mountains. Even whilst units were being moved into position, Wellesley had a narrow escape from death or capture. The British commander stood surveying the area from an isolated stone building, the Casa de Salinas, situated *en route* from the Alberche to the battlefield. Nearby were men of Donkin's brigade; no enemy threat seemed likely and these British troops were lolling in the welcome shade of olive groves. But a line of *tirailleurs* slipped over the Alberche, through the olive trees and up to the troops, closely followed by infantry battalions, and crept almost to the walls of the building in which Wellesley was talking to his staff. Just in time, the enemy were seen; rapid firing broke out; Wellesley and his staff ran headlong down the stairs, flung themselves upon their horses and galloped off with bullets humming around their ears. Donkin's brigade suffered 440 men killed, wounded and captured. At the same time a chance French shell exploded a Spanish powder magazine, flinging a gunner high in the air with his arms and legs outstretched like a frog. Omens for the battle seemed gloomy.

Worse was to come. Late in the afternoon French dragoons appeared opposite the Spanish divisions and, despite the 1,000-yard range, enjoyed themselves by popping off their pistols. The Spanish reaction seemed incredible: the whole front in this southern sector suddenly blazed away at the harmless enemy without waiting for

*Opposite* Wellesley leads his army back into Portugal and lures the French deep into the dangerous mountains.

orders, and even more remarkable was the infectious panic which now seized the Spanish units: troops started to break into flight, throwing away their arms and rushing and pushing to the rear. Wellesley stood only a hundred yards away.

Nearly 2,000 ran off [he reported to Castlereagh], who were neither attacked, nor threatened with an attack, and who were frightened only by the noise of their own fire; they left their arms and accoutrements on the ground, their officers went with them, and they . . . plundered the baggage of the British army.

At the time Wellesley merely commented: 'Look at the ugly hole those fellows have left.' Cuesta filled the gap with men from his second line and ordered two hundred of the captured deserters to be executed after the battle – Wellesley persuaded him to cut this number to forty.

And battle had still to start. By now the sun had begun to set, and although the French could be seen massing across the plain, it seemed too late in the day for large-scale attack. Troops looked forward to the welcome cool of the evening. But the night was to be infinitely hotter than the day: Victor was determined to take advantage of the upset caused by the precipitate flight of Spanish troops, and had ordered a bold attack during darkness. Just before 10 pm a whole French division slipped unseen and unopposed across the Portina, and split into three columns, each of three battalions. The centre column had been ordered to climb Medellin ridge by the direct route, while the north and south columns clambered up the two sides in a flanking movement. Night, which covered the enemy move, also led the centre column to veer too far south where it clashed into Hanoverian troops; the northern column lost itself and the southern only managed to exchange ineffectual long-range fire with British defenders. But the central battalions continued to lunge into the British lines, despite their off-course advance. Each side had difficulty in identifying the other; men fired from panic, and consternation spread to make the nature, extent, and direction of the attack hard to assess. General Sir Rowland Hill galloped to the fighting and barely managed to pull away from French skirmishers who grabbed at his horse; he then ordered his division into the counter-attack. His first troops were checked, but the 29th ran forward to engage the enemy while still in column formation; fierce fighting broke out at only forty yards' range; the French were pushed back and split into scattered groups as they retreated over the Portina, or were herded into captivity. Both sides lost just over three hundred men. Wellesley hurriedly rearranged his shaken troops as best he could in the darkness, then,

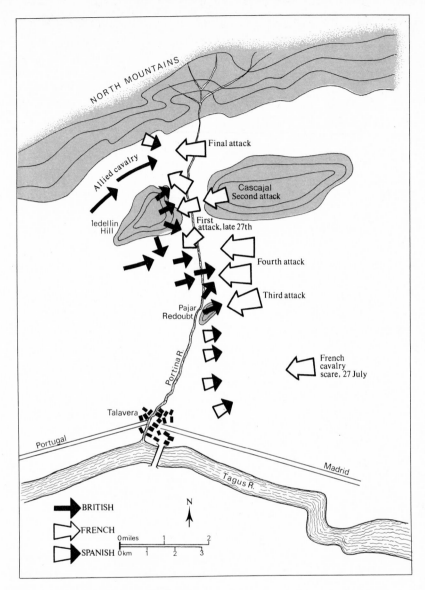

North Mountains

Final attack

Allied cavalry

Cascajal
Second attack

Iedellin
Hill

First
attack, late 27th

Fourth attack

Third attack

Pajar
Redoubt

Portina R.

French
cavalry
scare, 27 July

Talavera

Portugal

Madrid

Tagus R.

N

BRITISH

FRENCH

SPANISH

0 miles          1          2

0 km        1        2        3

Map 2    The Battle of
Talavera, July 1809.

after almost twenty hours on his feet or in the saddle, he wrapped
himself in his cloak and fell asleep.

Throughout the remainder of the night sporadic musket and
rifle fire spat in the darkness. At 5 am, 28 July, all chance of rest
was shattered by the sound of a single French gun blasting out from
the summit of the Cascajal ridge. Almost immediately other guns
opened up on the British positions, firing fast and accurate, and    93

Wellesley ordered his men to lie flat or take cover behind ridges. Morning mist, and the first smoke of battle, swirled above them.

Fog lay thicker along the Portina stream, and here French *tirailleurs* came forward to begin the ground attack against the line of light companies and riflemen positioned along the low bank. Mist restricted range and fighting took place at close quarters: with shadowy figures moving, running, crouching in the murk, muskets and rifles flashing, sudden screams and thuds and the flashing of bloody bayonets in the glimmering early morning sun. British skirmishers pulled back before the main French infantry; three enemy columns came after them, only a hundred yards behind, each composed of three battalions. Unlike the Vimiero tactics these columns were deployed in a wide, shallow formation, almost square-shaped, to give greater frontal firepower. One column headed towards the plain to the north of the Medellin ridge, the other two were directed at the ridge itself. The northernmost thrust was ineffectual, but the advances against the centre threatened the heart of the British positions, especially the area defended by brigades commanded by Stewart and Tilson. The former had deployed his men two deep in a line nine hundred yards long, enabling 1,500 muskets to be levelled upon the approaching enemy. On came the French, almost as if swaggering on parade: across the narrow Portina brook, up the slope, towards the waiting British. Now they were two hundred yards away. British troops could see the expressions on the faces of the enemy: some men could be seen talking, even laughing, others stared grimly to their front. Soon the gap closed to a hundred yards. British muskets were raised. Enemy drums ceased their steady throb; for a moment silence fell upon this section of the battlefield, until, at fifty yards, sharp commands rang out from both armies, muskets blazed, smoke billowed from barrels and over 1,000 bullets tore into the French. The column halted but stood firm and returned fire. Again came a disciplined British volley, then another. The French could be seen attempting to deploy into extended line but the gallant troops were dropping by the score. Another volley. More men flung up their arms, sagged and sprawled. Again came the crashing, murderous British fire. Ten volleys in all – over 10,000 bullets in less than three minutes. And no army in the world could have withstood such slaughter; the French turned and retreated with brave attempts to maintain reasonable order. The southern column, advancing against the junction of Stewart's right and Tilson's left, fared even worse from flank fire. Retreat slipped into confusion and the British commanders ordered immediate pursuit down the slopes and up to the stream, with Frenchmen flopping and dying or crawling with hideous wounds in vain search for safety. The first French infantry attack had finished; the time was just before 7 am.

Infantry firing dwindled, to be replaced by the heavy thuds of the artillery. This too subsided around 8.30 am and brooding silence settled over the ridge and over the plain. The sun rose higher and the heat became intense as the men stood in line waiting for the next onslaught. A tacit truce took place: first one soldier, then another, cautiously walked down to the polluted Portina to drink from the bloody water. Blue uniforms mingled with red with no sign of hatred or hostility; men talked in broken English or French and rudimentary sign-language, and laughed, slapped one another on the back, shared water canteens and pipe tobacco, until French drums beat an abrupt roll at 11 am to call troops back to battle again. Wellesley, standing by his horse at the summit of the Medellin, could see the enemy preparing for another attack, and at about noon on this sweltering day large dust-clouds could be seen behind the French lines: reinforcements were clearly approaching. Wellesley sent an aide to request extra troops from Cuesta and these arrived soon afterwards.

Shortly after 1 pm over eighty French guns opened fire. Then the enemy lines, perhaps as many as 30,000 men, began to move forward, first towards the Pajar redoubt at the extreme right of the British positions defended by Campbell's division. British skirmishers were sent scurrying back, but the French formations had been thrown into disorder by the rough terrain over which they had marched: olive groves, small enclosures and ditches. The attack was halted and broken by fierce British and Spanish artillery salvoes and rolling musket fire. But meanwhile the main French onslaught had been launched further north with 15,000 veterans crossing the open ground between the Pajar and the Medellin, screened by *tirailleurs* and extending over a three-quarter-mile front. Sherbrooke's division, outnumbered over two to one, stood ready to receive the blow. And once again the French were checked and held, and for the same reasons as before: the British troops were deployed in a two-deep line and could hence pour superior firepower into the packed French ranks, while the French, hampered from firing by their own men in front, were unable to expand from column to full line formation. Massive British volleys punctured the enemy ranks, and it mattered little that many of those British soldiers could hardly aim because of their shaking hands and heavy arms: sheer volume brought     95 destruction. French battalions wavered and fell apart, leaving the ground heaped high with dead and dying. Now British troops in Sherbrooke's division surged forward through the smoke in pursuit, cheering and firing as they ran – but the rigid British line consequently fell into disorder, and the enemy turned to deal with their pursuers. Survivors from the first French line ran back into the safety of the second and battalions were reformed with brilliant precision. Deadly fire swept the disorganised British; excitement and elation suddenly shifted to fear and consternation and the ragged British units suffered terrible casualties. Behind them, across the ground which they had previously held with such disciplined determination, stretched an ugly gap; French dragoons and artillery immediately started forward to take advantage.

Wellesley, cool as always, had already seen the danger. Terse orders were on their way, and all available troops were rushed into the breach. Men ran down the slopes of the Medellin, stumbling over rough ground, and took up hasty positions. They opened ranks to allow British survivors through, then stood ready, with no talking, no sound except their rapid breathing: a French officer wrote: 'The English. silent and impassive, with grounded arms, loomed like a long red wall; their aspect was imposing.' But the line comprised only about 3,000 men, and towards them were advancing over 10,000 French troops with 7,000 enemy horsemen ready to charge through any gap. If the line broke the entire Allied position would be toppled and total defeat made almost inevitable. The French were less than 150 yards away . . . 100 . . . 75 . . . And only then were orders rapped out. 'Make ready! Present! Fire!' With perfect cohesion and timing the redcoats discharged their volleys, loaded, fired, and riddled the advancing troops again, at regular fifteen-second intervals. The French commander, Lapisse, was struck down; some of his men staggered on, to be met with thrusting bayonets. The attack disintegrated and British cavalry hacked a way into the southern flank to send the French streaming back over the red-running Portina. No pursuit this time, only ringing cheers and hysterical shouts.

Another French thrust started to develop in the far north, in the largely undefended area on the opposite side of the Medellin, and Wellesley ordered a cavalry counter-attack: the 23rd Light Dragoons and the Hussars of the King's German Legion trotted out, formed line, and moved forward for the charge. They presented a magnificent spectacle as they cantered across the line below the watching troops on the Medellin: the plain seemed smooth and firm, almost like an exercise ground; pennants

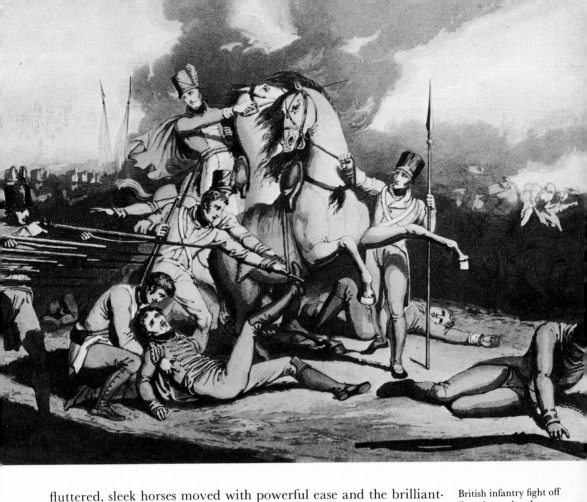

fluttered, sleek horses moved with powerful ease and the brilliant-uniformed riders held themselves proud and prepared. The tableau could have been one from a recruiting poster – but only for a few moments longer. Perhaps carried away by their own exultation and magnificence, the Light Dragoons gradually increased pace; the canter reached into a gallop; hooves drummed harder. Suddenly, immediately to their front, lay a fifteen-foot cleft in the ground concealed by long grass. Too late the dragoons tried to check the gallop and horses and riders hurtled into the cleft: for each cavalryman who managed to clear the gap, another was thrown violently down or ran full tilt into the far bank. Horses and riders lay screaming and struggling to rise, legs broken, necks shattered. Survivors streamed on at uncontrollable speed into the French squares. Only half the 23rd Light Dragoons returned to the British lines: the action had taken less than fifteen minutes. But at least the French advance in this sector had halted and the enemy columns now retired.

Firing dwindled to sporadic crackling along the length of the two armies; artillery thuds became less frequent; the Battle of

British infantry fight off French cavalry charges during the Battle of Talavera.

97

Talavera had finished. Three hours of daylight still remained, and the French were disorganised, but Wellesley decided an Allied pursuit would be foolhardy: his own divisions were weakened and he had insufficient trust in Cuesta's men to move them from defensive positions. 'The Spanish troops are not in a state of discipline to attempt a manoeuvre,' wrote Wellesley during the evening. With luck the battle would be resumed the following day and decisive defeat inflicted upon the enemy. As night fell units were being reformed and casualties counted – French losses were later found to be about 7,300 out of 40,000 compared with the British 5,400 out of 20,000. Wellesley had therefore lost a quarter of his force, compared with the enemy's eighteen per cent. But a numerically superior army had nevertheless been defeated.

And Marshal Victor had had enough. During the night he ordered his forces to retire; by dawn next day, 29 July, the French had gone, crossing the Alberche and heading east towards Toledo. They left behind a scene of terrible suffering spread over an area almost four miles long and two wide. Wellesley wrote to his brother William: 'I was hit but not hurt & my coat shot through. Almost all the Staff are wounded or have had their horses shot. Never was there such a Murderous Battle!' The resulting devastation was made worse by a fire which had started in the dry grass at six o'clock in the evening of the 28th, singeing or burning alive most of the badly wounded men who were unable to crawl away. Choking smoke billowed from the blaze and from burning wagons. Next morning the sights and sounds seemed even more horrible: the burning sun, the flies swarming in their thousands over the mutilated bodies and upon the faces of the helpless. Corpses were strewn everywhere, especially at the base of the Medellin hill and in and around Portina brook.

Here, indeed [wrote one eye-witness], the dead were so plentiful that it looked as if several battalions were merely sleeping there. Our own men could be distinguished by their red coats, and fifty paces off could be seen the blue and grey uniforms of the enemy.

French wounded begged for rescue from the marauding Spaniards who were intent upon cutting their throats.

We were particularly touched by a finely-built French grenadier who, sitting with philosophic composure amid the ruins of a powder chest containing grape shot that had blown up and smashed his leg above the ankle, greeted us in a friendly way. We gave him a gulp of wine from our bottles and comforted him.

Some men, who had received only comparatively minor wounds in the battle but who were incapable of walking, now lay dying of thirst, black tongues swelling from between cracked lips. French and English men lay together and whispered before they died. And everywhere were scattered slaughtered and wounded horses, and weapons, shattered carts, ammunition boxes, French shakos, helmets, bearskins, scraps of clothing, pouches and severed limbs. The more fortunate wounded had been taken to Talavera, where a convent had been turned into a ghastly operating theatre: amputated arms and legs were thrown in rapid succession from one upstairs window into a small square below, while outside the door waited a long groaning line of those still to be treated. Elsewhere, vigorous auctions were being held to sell off belongings of dead officers and men.

Almost two-thirds of Wellesley's small army were engaged in collecting, caring for, and burying the battle casualties. Clearly, rapid advance had to be out of the question, despite welcome reinforcements which had arrived on the 28th, just too late for the conflict itself. General Robert Crauford had brought his tough Light Division from Lisbon, marching at an incredible speed to cover the last forty-two miles in less than twenty-six hours – and this across central Spain in the July heat, with each man carrying up to sixty pounds on his back. Crauford lost less than two dozen stragglers out of a force of 2,500. But his men would now need to rest; the British army must stay where it was, despite the chance of an unopposed march upon Madrid. Within hours, this chance had slipped away. Wellesley remained heavily outnumbered, even by Victor's force alone, and now came a threat from the rear: disturbing reports started to arrive on 30 July of Soult's movement south from Galicia, threatening the communication link with Portugal. Moreover, the British were suffering from acute food shortages: for some days now troops had been on half-rations, and the Spaniards still refused to supply adequate provisions. Further serious news reached the British camp on 2 August: French forces, obviously from Soult's army, were reported to have taken Plasencia on the previous day, capturing British wounded and supplies. The life-line to Portugal had been severed; the French were massing both front and rear. An urgent conference took place between Wellesley and Cuesta later on the 2nd, at which the Spanish leader put forward a preposterous proposal to halve the Spanish and British forces, with one part advancing against Plasencia under Wellesley while he, Cuesta, marched on Madrid with the other. Wellesley wanted to be separated from his unreliable ally, and sug-  99 gested he should march either west or east if Cuesta went in the opposite direction. Agreement was finally reached that the British should move west against Soult, while Cuesta stayed behind to give rear support and to care for the British wounded.

The British army began to move before dawn, 3 August, amidst plaintive pleadings from the wounded not to be left behind – some tried to crawl after their marching comrades. Wellesley now had 18,000 men, including Crauford's Light Division: he knew little of enemy strength to his front but hoped Soult's forces had still to concentrate. Temporary reassurance came just before the British commander reached Oropesa at noon, when a local report indicated that the French force in Plasencia totalled only one corps. Soon afterwards a Spanish officer overtook Wellesley with a message from Cuesta, containing a captured French dispatch: the force in front of the tiny British army totalled not one but three French corps, numbering over 40,000 men. Cuesta, who was also threatened by Victor's army under the nominal command of King Joseph, was leaving Talavera to follow the British – thereby abandoning 1,500 British wounded.

The fate of the Peninsular War hung in the balance. From his experience so far Wellesley knew the regular Spanish army would be massacred by the French if no British support were given; the Spanish guerrillas, infinitely more valuable, could not secure victory alone. They had to have an efficient, professional army with which they could cooperate. The key to the whole situation therefore lay in the continued survival of the small British force. The army must remain in being if Spain was to be saved, even if this meant temporary retreat to the Portuguese frontier. Wellesley realized he had to feint, slip away, dodge and outwit the superior forces which threatened to surround him. The war had to be one of manoeuvre, in many ways far more difficult, dangerous and exhausting than a pitched battle. And already the troops were nearing starvation.

First, Sir Arthur Wellesley halted at Oropesa. Temporary safety had to be secured by crossing the Tagus at nearby Arzobispo, thus putting the broad river between the British and the bulk of the French. Cuesta arrived at Oropesa on 4 August and argued for a battle rather than moving south over the river; Wellesley knew this could be disastrous: a defeat north of the Tagus could mean total annihilation, and even if Soult merely kept the Allies occupied, time would be allowed for the approach of King Joseph's army from the west. The British army therefore started to cross the bridge and ford at Arzobispo during the night of the 4th, and the Spaniards followed after twenty-four hours' hesitation, leaving a strong force to guard the crossing. The British laboured their way towards Almarez and the Portuguese frontier over rough roads which often had to be widened to allow gun passage. Men were already collapsing from lack of food, while a few of the more fortunate still had mutton legs skewered onto their bayonets. Soult forced the Arzobispo crossing late on the 7th, routing the 6,000 Spanish defenders, and Wellesley wrote to his brother William on the 8th that he now had 'the whole host of (French) Marshals' against him – Soult, Ney, Mortier, Victor, Sebastiani, Jourdan and Kellerman – and he added: 'We have suffered much from want of Provisions.' Once again Wellesley showed himself highly critical of the men under his command:

The British army is a bad one for a retreat or for any privations; and I really believe that in every respect with the exception of the Guards & one or two other Corps this is the worst British army that ever was in the field.

Such condemnation was hardly justified: conditions were fast becoming intolerable for his troops, who were having to eat whatever scraps they could scrounge: goat's offal had to be bought from Spanish peasants for four dollars a piece, or double the amount the complete animal would normally be worth. The heat remained intense: soldiers stuck olive leaves or pieces of paper on their underlips to prevent them from bursting. Water became so scarce that men thought nothing of lying with their faces almost completely submerged in any foul, muddy pool they could find, even though leeches crawled into their nostrils and mouths. And Wellesley fully realised the Spaniards were to blame for much of the hardship; a letter from Cuesta on the 10th, accusing British troops of plunder, received a stern reply from the British commander next morning.

It will be impossible for me to remain any longer in a country in which no arrangement has been made for the supply of provisions; and in which it is understood that all the provisions . . . are to be supplied solely and exclusively to the use of the Spanish troops.

Next day, 12 August, Cuesta suffered a paralytic stroke which left him crippled and obliged him to resign. Neither of the two Spanish generals whom Wellesley would have liked to see as Cuesta's successor, La Romana or Castaños, received the appointment, which was eventually given to General Carlos Areizaga, a man of doubtful military skill. But at least the British army now

held a stronger position after the hard days of marching:
Crauford held the Tagus crossings at Almarez while Wellesley's
main force stretched further west and the Spaniards were deployed in nearby defensive lines. The Tagus could be crossed by the
French farther east and west, but Soult would then have to
advance through harsh delaying country.

An uneasy stalemate had therefore been reached. The French
could not hold all parts of Spain simultaneously; nor could they
inflict decisive defeat upon the British and Spanish main armies
in their present positions, and Soult soon marched north to re-take
the area he had been obliged to leave three weeks before.
Wellesley, on the other hand, had to move to find supplies, and
ordered a march south towards Merida and Badajoz, where he
could establish contact with the Portuguese border fortress at
Elvas and thereby obtain provisions. Crauford's rearguard left
Almarez on 20 August, leaving the position in Spanish hands, and
the condition of the British army as a whole can be judged by the
performance of this one division: only a few weeks before,
Crauford's men had covered over forty miles in a single march,
yet now they could stagger no more than three without having to
stop for urgent rest. But Wellesley had managed to preserve his
army reasonably intact. His skilful manoeuvring had enabled his
forces to survive for the next offensive. And on the 26th he had
further cause for celebration, although the news would take three
weeks to reach him: on this day he was elevated to the peerage. His
brother William selected a title for him in his absence – Viscount
Wellington of Talavera and of Wellington, and Baron Douro of
Welleslie in the County of Somerset. The honour was gazetted on
4 September but not until 16 September would the new Lord
sign himself Wellington for the first time. His elder brother
Richard had also received fresh recognition: during August he
succeeded Frere as British Ambassador at Seville. He immediately
pressed his brother to keep his army in Spain, rather than withdrawing into Portugal. The British commander was reluctant to
oblige. 'My opinion,' he wrote to his other brother William from
Merida, 'is that in the existing state of their affairs we (the Army I
mean) ought to have nothing to say to the Spaniards.'

Wellington did however consent to remain at Badajoz for a
while, just inside Spain, and there he halted on 3 September, still
determined not to enter into a joint operation with his Allies.
Instead he started secret preparations for further withdrawal. The
commander slipped from the British HQ early in September and
reached Lisbon on the 10th; the next weeks were spent in a close

examination of the surrounding area and especially of the rugged region north to Torres Vedras, and by 20 October a detailed and highly secret memorandum had been completed, which would be put into startling effect almost exactly a year later. While in Lisbon, Wellington spared time to criticise the riotous behaviour of young officers there, writing to the British Governor on 26 October:

My dear Sir, I am concerned to be obliged to inform you, that it has been mentioned to me that British officers who are in Lisbon are in the habit of going to the theatres, where some of them conduct themselves in a very improper manner, much to the annoyance of the public, and to the injury of the proprietors and of the performers . . . Officers of the army can have nothing to do behind the scenes, and it is very improper that they should appear upon the stage during the performance . . .

By mid-November Wellington had returned to his army at Badajoz, and almost immediately news from central Spain confirmed the wisdom of his recent visit to Lisbon. The new Spanish military leader, Carlos Areizaga, had been ordered to march on Madrid with 56,000 men: the Central Junta at Seville had become over-confident, and still hoped the British would march in support, especially if Areizaga scored some successes. Instead he suffered catastrophic defeat at Ocaña on 19 November, losing 18,000 men. Ten days later another Spanish army under the Duke del Parque was routed at Alba de Tormes.

Spain's regular forces were shattered and a British retreat into Portugal seemed even more necessary. But one advantage derived from the disintegration of the Spanish armies: the best of the troops slipped away to join irregular bands of marauding guerrillas. The Spaniards were never lacking in individual courage, and in guerrilla warfare this could be exploited to the full. The French could be harassed and pinned down by a force which melted away as soon as enemy columns approached; and the French could only retaliate by brutal repression which in turn persuaded an increasing number of locals to turn against the invaders. Guerrilla warfare had begun in Aragon against Suchet's troops and where a direct threat could be imposed upon the French communications; operations had spread to neighbouring Catalonia, with local forces attacking the link between Perpignan and the French base at Barcelona. Partisans had only been quietened after extensive counter-operations involving thousands of French troops, and the invaders were soon to find that when one area had been brought under apparent control another would burst into activity. More and more French troops would be needed, so reducing numbers available to deal with the British army. Wellington wrote to Lord Liverpool: 'It is probable that, although the armies may be lost and the principal Juntas and authorities of the provinces may be dispersed, the war of partisans may continue.' Napoleon's Spanish ulcer was beginning to fester.

But another side existed to this situation. Napoleon remained victorious in northern and central Europe, and the Treaty of Schönbrunn, signed on 14 October as a result of the Battle of Wagram, stamped the seal on this supremacy, thus allowing the Emperor to shift further forces to the Peninsula. Wellington's primary task under his original orders was to protect Portugal and nothing more, at the moment, could anyway be done in Spain. On 29 January 1810, the Central Junta abdicated; forty-eight hours later King Joseph entered Seville. Napoleon was expected to take personal command during the spring. Wellington had to prepare for even harder campaigns in the new year. The British army had already moved over the border and the commander had established his HQ high in the central Portuguese mountains at Viseu. The Portuguese had been called to arms with one of their infantry brigades incorporated into each British division. Intensive training continued during the foul February weather Meanwhile Wellington prepared for further retreat, and, having received authority from the Portuguese governing council, issued drastic orders to local authorities: the country was to be defended by a combination of a harsh scorched earth policy and the activities of the local Portuguese militia, the *Ordenanza*. Food, mills and bridges must be destroyed in the face of a French advance; livestock must be slaughtered or removed; crops must be spoilt or otherwise denied to the enemy. All healthy men between the ages of sixteen and sixty would be conscripted into the *Ordenanza*, to fight with whatever weapons were available. The British army would block the French advance where possible, but rather than take undue risks it would gradually fall back upon the capital. Contact would however be maintained with the advancing army.

So, as the short soft spring fingered up from the Portuguese lowlands into the mountains around Viseu, Wellington began his daring cat-and-mouse tactics to lure the French from Spain and away from the guerrillas. A single mistake could lead to terrible disaster, as illustrated by the sudden threat to the British rearguard in March. Crauford's men were positioned between Almeida and the lower Agueda, reinforced by two Portuguese battalions to make 4,000 men and six guns. Units were ordered to maintain constant alert: only seven minutes were needed to bring this highly trained division under arms in the middle of the night, and fifteen

to bring it in order of battle to the alarm-posts, with baggage

Sir Arthur Wellesley
initially sailed to the
Peninsular eighth in
order of command. After
his success at Vimiero
he returned home, then
travelled to Portugal
again in spring, 1809—
this time in supreme
command. He did not
come back to England
until the war had ended;
and by then he had won
fame and honour, and
enjoyed the title
Viscount Wellington of
Talavera, Baron Douro
of Welleslie. *From the
painting by Goya*

An allegorical painting by an unknown artist, depicting the military alliance between Britain, Portugal and Spain. Framed by the three flags are the Spanish and Portuguese monarchs with the Prince of Wales in the centre. On the white horse is Wellington, with his friend and subordinate general, Beresford, riding beside him.

The mounting terror of guerrilla warfare, depicted by Goya, from which Wellington reaped massive benefits.

removed to the rear. Even this speed proved barely sufficient when a lightning French attack was launched during darkness on 19 March. About six hundred enemy grenadiers under General Ferey darted forward, making use of the black shadows cast by the bright moonlight, and within seconds the outlying British sentries had been stabbed, and the French threw themselves on the picquets even before the alarm could be sounded. Noise of firing and shouting alerted nearby troops and they rushed into the battle without attempting to form line. Hand-to-hand fighting continued for over an hour until the French were forced back.

Over the border the main French army would soon be ready for advance. Wellington had prepared himself as best he could, but his confidence sadly failed to be reflected among ministers back at home. The Government had still to recover from the disastrous expedition to the Netherlands the previous summer, when 40,000 men under the command of the Earl of Chatham – the Younger Pitt – had sailed in an attempt to take Antwerp. Precious time had been spent capturing Flushing, and the French had been given opportunity to reinforce the Dutch capital. Chatham had been obliged to sail for home, leaving a garrison of 15,000 on Walcheren Island, of whom 7,000 died of malaria. The Government were anxious to avoid a similar fiasco in the Peninsula, and the Walcheren episode reduced the number of reinforcements which Wellington might otherwise have received. Lord Liverpool, now at the War Office, sent hesitant advice to Wellington on 27 February, symbolic of the Government's wavering attitude: they did not want to be accused of deserting Portugal, nor could they risk another humiliating British defeat; the burden of responsibility consequently remained on Wellington's shoulders. Everything, wrote Liverpool, must be left to Wellington's discretion, but 'the safety of the British army in Portugal is the first object which His Majesty has in view'; at the same time, Wellington should not evacuate Portugal until 'absolutely necessary'. Further communications during the next weeks echoed a similar fear by ministers that Wellington would find himself trapped and defeated or would take undue risks. The British commander penned a long letter to Lord Liverpool, dated 2 April 1810, from Viseu, in which he gave a clear report of his coming strategy. He remained convinced he could both protect Britain's ally and keep his army safe.

The great disadvantage under which I labour is, that Sir John Moore, who was here before me, gave an opinion that this country could not be defended by the army under his command . . . I have as much respect as any man can have for the opinion and judgement of Sir John Moore . . . But he positively knew nothing of Portugal, and could know nothing of its existing state . . . My opinion is, that as long as we shall remain in a state of activity in Portugal, the contest must continue in Spain; that the French are most desirous that we should withdraw from the country, but know that they must employ a very large force indeed in the operations which will render it necessary for us to go away.

Such a force would expose 'their whole fabric in Spain to great risk'. So, while he agreed the army should be evacuated if the worst happened, that time had still to come.

Depend upon it, whatever people may tell you, I am not so desirous as they imagine of fighting desperate battles . . . But I have kept the army for six months in two positions, notwithstanding their own desire, and that of the allies, that I should take advantage of many opportunities which the enemy apparently offered.

Wellington later believed that only his determined attitude prevented the Government from ordering a withdrawal from Portugal. 'It is quite certain,' he wrote many years afterwards, 'that my opinion alone was the cause of the continuance of the war in the Peninsula.'

The enemy might occupy the twin capitals of Madrid and Seville; they might swamp the country with troops – 324,996 had arrived by February; but they had still to gain victory. Guerrillas were everywhere; Cadiz, reinforced by a strong British garrison, still held out; Portugal was being prepared to absorb the shock of a French advance. Napoleon, who had declared on 4 December that 'when I shall show myself beyond the Pyrenees the frightened leopard [Wellington] will fly to the ocean to avoid shame, defeat and death,' now wisely decided not to take personal command. Besides, he was preoccupied with divorcing the barren but much-loved Josephine and marrying the Austrian Emperor's daughter, Marie-Louise, in order to sire a son; and ominous rumblings of war with Russia were beginning to be heard. On 18 May reports therefore reached Wellington, still at Viseu, that Marshal André Masséna, Prince of Essling, had been given the command of a 138,000-strong army with orders to drive the British into the sea. The swarthy Masséna was later described by Wellington as the ablest general after Napoleon among those who opposed him.

Masséna reached Salamanca on 28 May. The French campaign had already begun with the surrender of the Spanish garrison at Astorga on 22 April. On 26 April a second and infinitely more important Spanish fortress, Ciudad Rodrigo, had been surrounded, although the siege operations were delayed until 30 May. This fortress stood astride the northern corridor into Portugal via the Douro river, and even before Masséna's arrival Wellington barely resisted the temptation to advance and drive the French from the area. Temptation was offered again by the crafty Masséna in early June: only 26,000 men were left to besiege the fortress – sufficiently small, hoped the French commander, to lure Wellington forward. Once again the British commander refused to sniff the bait, despite taunts from the French, Spanish pleas, and increasing criticism from his own officers and men. Wellington knew that even small losses would seriously reduce any chances of defending Portugal – and would give further and perhaps final inducement to ministers at home to end British participation in the war. Yet the Spanish garrison fought with desperate bravery, and the Governor, Herrasti, sent a contemptuous refusal to a French call to surrender at the end of June; on 1 July further enemy siege-works were constructed and the end was clearly imminent; on 9 July French fire increased to terrible proportions, Spanish guns were silenced and part of the town became a raging inferno. A pitiful note reached British lines from Herrasti: 'Oh come now, now, to the succour of this place!' Next day, after 40,000 French shells had exploded within the city walls and barely a house remained undamaged, the garrison surrendered and Herrasti handed his sword to Ney, the French local commander, who gallantly passed it back again.

The next target would clearly be Almeida, the Portuguese

fortress opposite to Ciudad Rodrigo on the banks of the river Coa. Ney started to cross the frontier in the third week of July, and the battle for Portugal had begun. Conflict started in unfortunate fashion for the British. General Crauford had been ordered to cover the French advance to the Coa, but to avoid becoming entangled; the British rearguard commander, who had been acting with contemptuous audacity against French outlying detachments, now almost over-reached himself on 24 July when he placed his Light Division against virtually the whole of Ney's advancing corps. One of the participants wrote afterwards: 'I consider it little short of a miracle that a single British soldier survived.' By the stormy evening of the 24th Crauford had deployed his 4,000 infantry and 1,100 cavalry in an oblique line towards the Coa with the left almost at the walls of Almeida. Vivid lightning lit the sodden troops and the glistening guns; the French were known to be advancing rapidly, but still Crauford refused to retire. Dawn broke wet on the 25th and with it came a massive attack by the French, outnumbering the British at least four to one. Only brilliant handling of individual units by the various commanders averted total defeat.

The conflict was tremendous [wrote the eye-witness]. Thrice we repulsed the enemy at the point of the bayonet . . . At length the bugle sounded for retreat: just then, my left-hand man, one of the stoutest in the regiment, was hit by a musket shot – he threw his head back, and was instantly dead. I fired at the fellow who shot my comrade; and before I could re-load my pay-sergeant, Thomas, received a ball in the thigh, and earnestly implored me to carry him away. As the enemy was not far off, such a load was by no means desirable: but he was my friend . . .

The Light Division withdrew over the Coa, leaving three hundred behind. Almeida had to be left surrounded and alone, but the French moved cautiously, holding fire until 26 August. Wellington, delighted by this delay, further hoped the fortress defence would allow the main British army to withdraw, possibly holding back the French until the autumn rains came to bog down the enemy advance. The Portuguese garrison was strong, commanded by a British officer, Colonel Cox, and ample supplies of ammunition and food had been stocked inside the stronghold. For the first few hours after the siege began on the 26th, the defenders fought back bravely. Then, soon after dark, a massive explosion ripped up into the sky, the ground trembled and a mighty roar could be heard for miles around. Powder had been piled in the cathedral; one of the kegs had leaked while being carried to this improvised magazine, and a chance shell had ignited the thin trail which had been left. The trail led to the cathedral, and the whole

store erupted. About five hundred men were blown apart in that single second, the cathedral collapsed in a tremendous mass of rubble and only six houses were left standing. Essential ammunition had been lost, and the demoralised Portuguese forced Cox to surrender on the 28th. Masséna was now free to advance.

Part of old Almeida, scene of the massive explosion on 26 August 1810, which led to the garrison's premature surrender.

The next few days passed in extreme tension. Only the small British army and the Portuguese partisans stood in the way of the French offensive: Wellington knew that if his army were defeated the entire Peninsula might be lost. A precipitate retreat would be safer, but would leave the French entirely free to their own devices. Contact must therefore be maintained, and if possible a battle fought on ground of Wellington's own choosing. But he must avoid the dreadful danger of being outflanked. As September opened the French forces were concentrated for the advance – but which road would this march follow? Wellington sent brave scouts to operate behind enemy lines: knowledge of the enemy route was essential if contact was to be kept and a swift enveloping manoeuvre prevented. Masséna could move west from Almeida and use the northern corridor into Portugal, or he could strike further south via Castelo Branco, or he could attempt a combination of both. And, if the northern route was selected, a further complication arose through the existence of two roads between Almeida and Coimbra, one north and the other south of the Mondego river, although British staff officers considered this north road to Coimbra to be an unlikely choice: the track, in atrocious condition, ran through rugged country which would give the *Ordenanza* full opportunity for ambush and sniping tactics.

Wellington massed his forces on the Mondego, to be in a central position.

I have made all my dispositions for falling back [he wrote to his brother William on the 5th], and [I am] collecting my army; and when that is done I shall act according to my own view of the circumstances of the moment. The enemy is exceedingly cautious; they risk nothing; and I think they are scarcely strong enough, even in their own opinion, for the attainment of their object.

Underlying this confidence ran the tense strain to which both the army and the commander were subjected. The hours before action are always the most nerve-wracking; many of the officers in Wellington's army wanted to move into attack, and even urged an advance into Spain. Grumbling became louder. Wellington had already reacted to this opposition with a display of peevishness on the 29th in a letter to Colonel Torrens in London.

Really when I reflect upon the characters and attainments of some of the General Officers of this army, and consider that these are the persons on whom I am to rely to lead my columns against the French Generals, and who are to carry my instructions into execution, I tremble; and, as Lord Chesterfield said of the Generals of his day, 'I only hope that when the enemy reads the list of their names he trembles as I do.'

Now, on 5 September, he told William that he had 'terrible disadvantages' to contend with. 'The army was, and indeed is still, the worst British army that was ever sent from England . . . but still I don't despair.' Wellington added: 'I am positively in no scrape.' Yet this 'scrape' would soon occur if accurate intelligence did not arrive concerning the enemy's next move, and for the next anxious days Wellington was engaged in studying all available evidence – and in quarrelling with the Portuguese authorities over an Allied plan of action. On 11 September the British commander exploded again in a letter to Stuart, now British minister in Lisbon. 'The temper of some of the officers of the British army gives me more concern than the folly of the Portuguese Government . . . there is a system of croaking in the army.'

Masséna would have been well advised to delay his move as long as possible: dissension and consequent demoralisation would have increased in the British camp. Instead, the French commander selected his route, and by 17 September Wellington had clear indications that this advance would not only be restricted to the northern route, but would also take the inferior road between Almeida and Coimbra. 'There are certainly many bad roads in Portugal,' wrote a delighted Wellington to Stuart on the 18th, 'but the enemy has decidedly taken the worst.' Wellington hurriedly switched his forces towards this unexpected move. Not only would Masséna's mistake cause suffering to his troops from the rugged terrain, from vicious guerrilla tactics by the Portuguese partisans and from the scorched earth policy, but it would also enable Wellington to fight a battle on his ground. The 'croakers' might be silenced.

For three arduous days the French advanced from Almeida, via Viseu, towards Bussaco. Peasants, born and bred in the mountains, kept up a twenty-four-hour harassment: sentries were found with throats sliced from ear to ear, stragglers were tortured and left to die in agony, and throughout each day's marching boulders were constantly flung down upon the columns and musket fire echoed through the narrow passes. Wagons had to be abandoned with axles and wheels splintered by the rutted track; gun carriages had to be hauled up sharp inclines; supplies had to be thrown away when they became too cumbersome. Yet food and provisions were almost impossible to find in the neighbouring countryside. By 19 September Masséna had managed to reach Mortagoa, eight miles from Bussaco, where he delayed until the 24th – according to the rumours this resulted from his mistress crying out for rest. British troops waited nervously for the retreat to continue, never knowing when the enemy might suddenly lurch forward again and perhaps catch them unawares. Men in the rearguard, camped in a scented pine-wood on the night of the 22nd, were suddenly stricken by unaccountable panic.

No enemy was near [reported one of the soldiers], nor was any alarm given, yet suddenly large bodies of the troops started from sleep, as if seized with a phrenzy, and dispersed in every direction; some climbed the trees, they knew not why.

Order was only restored when one quick-thinking officer shouted a deliberately incorrect warning that French cavalry were about to attack: the soldiers fell into line mechanically.

Late on the 24th the enemy began to move again. French advance forces were lured down the track to Coimbra, rather than taking the easier road northwards to Oporto, and the bulk of the army followed on the 25th – towards waiting British troops positioned at Bussaco. Wellington had prepared his battle.

The road from Mortagoa split into two tracks, both of which had to cross the long, narrow Bussaco ridge stretching ten miles south to the Mondego river, dominating the valley to the east and giving excellent defensive positions although with the terrain varying in height. Wellington had ordered a track to be built along the summit to allow good communication between troops deployed along it. By 10 am on 26 September, Wellington's army was already in position, concentrated in the northern sector of the ridge across which ran the Mortagoa roads: the northern five miles were held by 8,500 men per mile compared with 3,000 per mile further south. Most of the troops were concealed behind the crest, and Wellington gave orders during the 26th that no fires were to be lit after dark. The restriction was imposed more to confuse the enemy than to preserve secrecy: by the evening of the 26th Masséna knew the British were deployed in the area, and vigorous probing had started. Over to the east the usual heavy dust-clouds indicated the main enemy advance, while French skirmishers filtered into the deep ravines on the fringe of the ridge. Night fell: rifles snapped in the dark chasms at the base of the rise, while thousands of French bivouac fires flickered and flared in the wooded countryside beyond.

Towards dawn these fires, clustered in three main groups, each indicating the whereabouts of a French corps, were blotted out to the watching British by early morning fog. Mist made lone British sentries seem like mysterious phantoms as they paced the ridge, and also allowed the French *tirailleurs* to creep up the lower slopes. The British army stood to arms at 4 am. For two tense hours the soldiers waited. Skirmishing fire suddenly increased. And soon afterwards, French battalions burst through the lifting fog towards Picton's division, almost in the centre of the ridge. The first thrust retired after suffering heavy artillery fire, but a second attack consisting of eleven battalions had already developed a mile to the north, first against Lightburne's brigade on Picton's extreme left, then swerving slightly south after the French had received vigorous Allied fire in their flank. Their new direction would lead them to a weaker section in the British line held by troops under Major Gwynn. Tough Irishmen under Colonel Alexander Wallace rushed forward to give support – but this would still only give a strength of four against the eleven French battalions. Wallace found time for a quiet talk to his men as the enemy advanced up the slopes towards them. 'Now, Connaught Rangers, mind what you are going to do . . . When I bring you face to face with those French rascals, drive them down the hill – don't give the false touch, but push home to the muzzle!' He finished his briefing with the French only a hundred yards away. 'I have nothing more to say, for in a minute or two there'll be such an infernal noise about your ears that you won't be able to hear yourselves.' And, without waiting for the French to finish clambering up the slope, he ordered his men to meet them. The unleashed Irishmen leapt yelling upon the French, weary from their climb up the boulder-strewn hillside. The first ranks were thrown bodily on to those behind; the lines wavered and began to topple. The thick mass of Frenchmen retreated, Irish bayonets plunging into their backs, their flanks swept by musket volleys, and with cannonballs thudding into their midst. Down the hill they streamed. Wellington, wearing a plain low hat, grey overcoat, white collar and a light sword, galloped up to the triumphant, panting Irishmen. ''Pon my honour, Wallace, I never witnessed a more gallant charge.'

Two French assaults had been repulsed and the wet rocks were already red with blood. Wounded men shrieked and moaned amongst the boulders, and equipment and weapons littered the shredded grass. But some survivors from the first attack still clung to the higher slopes, exchanging long-range fire with the defenders, and, at 7 am, the French tried again. Two new columns, totalling seven battalions, worked their way up the slopes against Picton's division – Picton himself, still wearing his night-cap, was almost hoarse from shouting commands. The northern column, commanded by General Foy, forced a way to the summit and Frenchmen rushed cheering towards the valuable road which ran along the length of the ridge. Wellington's troops managed to reach this track first. Men from Leith's division, and from Hill's even further south, advanced rapidly up the pathway and plunged into the French. Foy's battalions were in disorder after their climb; superbly controlled British volleys once again sent the enemy reeling and fleeing down to the plain. More shattered bodies were flung across the slopes. Masséna had hoped these three assaults would strike through Wellington's line and then wheel to the north to take the bulk of the Allied army in the rear. At the same time Ney's corps would strike further north, taking the village of Sula and advancing rapidly along the narrow but well-paved road towards Bussaco convent. Defending the latter area were Crauford's Light Division and Pack's Independent Portuguese Brigade. Now, at about 8.15 am, Ney's first troops began their bid for glory

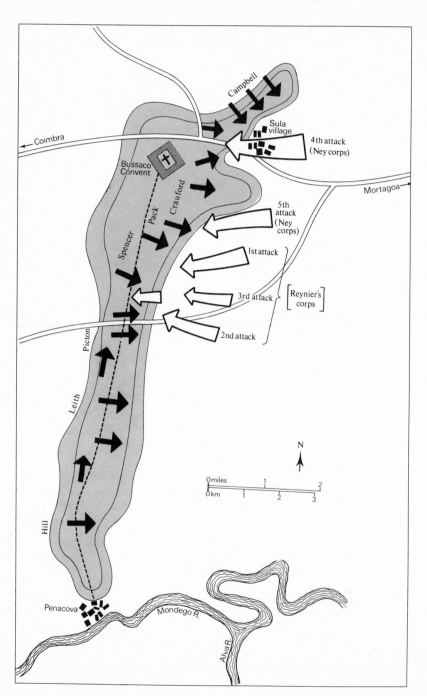

Map 3   The Battle of
Bussaco, September
1810.

under the command of Loison, despite the failure of the linked French assaults in the centre.

Portuguese troops in and around Sula gave ground and re-treated back up the hill. The French swept on, suffering heavy artillery fire but apparently heading towards an area largely undefended by British infantrymen – the enemy could see no signs of significant troop concentrations to their front. On they went, driving British skirmishers from boulder to boulder. The columns wound up the slopes, and the skirmishers retreated over the top, breathless and begrimed with powder. British guns were pulled back. Only a few yards remained to the summit, and the French were already cheering. But immediately over the crest waited Crauford's 1,800 crack troops. Abruptly 'Black Bob' jumped on to a boulder, swept off his hat and screamed to his men. 'Now! Now! Avenge Sir John Moore! Charge!' A mighty shout burst from the troops as they rose from cover, and the first volley splattered into the French at only five yards: faces and bodies were blown apart, and three times the muskets fired before the British hacked and bayoneted their way into the shocked, stumbling French ranks. Both enemy flanks were lapped by the wings of Crauford's division, blue uniforms gushed red and down went the French with the frenzied British thrusting into their midst. Mutilated carcasses marked the ghastly line of retreat. Yet even now the brave French kept trying. About forty minutes later, at 9 am, Ney's corps attempted another push further south against Pack's Portuguese. A pine wood on the lower slopes was success-fully cleared, then the French left the trees and began to scramble up towards the crest. They saw Portuguese brown uniforms in front of them instead of British red coats, and this gave them added courage. But the Portuguese proved as effective as their Allies: volley after volley hissed down into the French and the enemy retreated before this tornado of bullets.

Skirmishing continued throughout the morning and afternoon, but the battle had ended. The French suffered over 4,500 casualties in just over four hours. Wellington had lost 1,252, split equally between British and Portuguese. Soldiers stayed in their positions for the rest of the 27th. At about 2 pm troops from both armies gathered to draw water at a small stream running near the base of the ridge, and British and Frenchmen chatted as though nothing had happened. Equally incongruous was the sight of a lone and beautiful Portuguese girl who drove her ass, loaded with her belongings, through the British lines, across the corpse-strewn battlefield, and on through the French.

British troops suddenly
emerge from cover to
fire point-blank into the
French lines during the
struggle near Bussaco
convent.

The Allies suffered a sudden threat during the afternoon of the
following day, the 28th, when French detachments worked their
way round the ridge to the north. Wellington hurriedly ordered
the retreat to be resumed and the Allied army slipped away during
the night, leaving deceptive bivouac fires. Masséna, despite the
wounds to his army, ordered rapid advance: he believed he had
Wellington on the run; Wellington, with his secret plans well
prepared, knew better. But for all the commander's preparations,
retreat still caused hardships. The French were close behind when
the Allies passed through Coimbra on 1 October and already stores
were being abandoned. Troops reached Condacia the same day,
where more supplies were destroyed – the streets ran ankle-deep in
rum, into which soldiers dipped their mugs to help themselves as
they marched. Commissariat officers handed out shoes and shirts
which would otherwise have been left behind: years later, in a
spate of useless bureaucratic energy, the commissariat called for a
return off the men who had received these free items. Meanwhile
the scorched earth policy became increasingly evident, with

consequent suffering for the Portuguese. Most preferred to flee rather than face the French. They had to leave behind most of their belongings, but tried to drive animals and poultry with them: roads became blocked by squealing pigs, squawking hens and screeching Portuguese peasants. The German officer August Schaumann described the scene:

At one moment an old grandmother, riding a donkey, supported by two old women, could be seen passing through the throng, and a little later she was knocked down by a mule bearing a load of camp kettles, and, amid piteous cries, tramped under foot. Ladies, who, according to the custom of the country, had perhaps never left their homes except to go to Mass, could be seen walking along, hand in hand, three in a row, wearing silk shoes.

Monks and nuns who had fled their monasteries and convents were wandering aimlessly, and mingling with the crowd were prisoners released by the British from Condacia jail. The retreat became increasingly confused, despite breathing space given by Masséna's pause at Coimbra on 2 and 3 October: gun carriages had to be forced through the throng; roads were strewn with smashed cases, broken vehicles and dead horses. The noise grew tremendous: wailing women, now with their fine silk shoes split and blood-stained, crying babies, screeching carts, swearing men – and the infuriating sound of Portuguese muleteers 'singing the long notes of their Hymn to the Virgin Mary through their noses'. The streets of Leira, reached on the 3rd, soon became greasy with spilt coffee, sugar, chocolate, corn and flour, rags and broken crockery: British troops joined local criminals in looting, despite stern measures taken by Wellington – a soldier at Coimbra, caught in the act of stealing a huge gilded mirror, had been strung up by the roadside, with his swinging corpse reflecting in his would-be loot hanging beside him.

Behind the British swept the marauding French. Rearguard actions were fought on the 7th, 8th and 9th by Crauford's indefatigable Light Division, and the Portuguese *Ordenanza* slipped in to massacre the enemy wherever they could, moving round behind Masséna's force to sever communications with Spain. Masséna seemed unaware of this isolation. In front of him lay promise of a glorious victory: either the British would be brought to final battle, or they would be hurled into the sea. Supremely confident dispatches were sent back to Napoleon; most never found their way through the partisans. And even as the rearguard actions were being fought on the 8th and 9th the main Allied army moved into the brilliantly prepared positions – the lines of the Torres Vedras. The snarling British leopard could now turn in his tracks. ⟩————— 119

# Chapter 6

# Road
# to Fuentes

Autumn rains began to flood the dusty Portuguese countryside during the evening of 8 October. Tracks ran with red mud which splattered soldiers, civilians and horses, and thunderstorms massed heavy over the hills as the Allied army took up positions in the fortified lines. Rivers rose to break bridges, and the French advance slowed. Before Masséna now loomed an impenetrable defensive network instead of glorious victory. Wellington's plans had envisaged a number of alternative schemes for the Torres Vedras positions. He now decided to hold the northernmost line from the mouth of the Zizandre on the surf-swept Atlantic coast to Alhandra on the Tagus, originally intended to provide outposts for the main line based on Mafra.

The defensive system stretched twenty-six miles and consisted of linked hill forts and numerous redoubts covering the passes through to Lisbon. Maximum use had been made of ridge contours, arcs of fire were carefully measured and communication links were laid for speedy reinforcements. A semaphore system enabled messages to be flagged from the Atlantic to the Tagus in seven minutes. The network would not be defended by Wellington's main army, but by 25,000 Portuguese militia, 8,000 Spanish troops under Romana, and 2,500 British artillerymen and marines. The Royal Navy would protect the sea flanks. The principal British and Portuguese regular units were deployed behind the lines, ready to concentrate against a French thrust, and, as regiments arrived between 8 and 10 October, they were led to allotted positions. Wellington established his HQ at Pero Negro, with the bulk of the army on either side. Behind the defences stretched five hundred square miles of safe Portuguese territory, sufficient to supply the army and the refugees. Wellington believed Masséna would either have to assault or starve.

In mid-October the enemy massed and seemed about to attack, and indeed probing took place on the 14th. Then activity dwindled again; the British army was allowed to celebrate George III's birthday – the fiftieth year of his reign – in peace on 25 October, while Masséna sat in his HQ and planned his next move, and Wellington puzzled over the lack of enemy offensive attempts. By 14 November Masséna's preparations were complete. Straw dummies were left to deceive British outposts and the French army withdrew under cover of fog, back thirty miles to positions stretching fifteen miles between Santarem and Rio Maior, well-protected by earthworks and marshes. The 'crafty old fox'

*Opposite* A satirical French engraving of a British courier – the link in Wellington's comprehensive communication chain behind the defensive positions.

121

Masséna had been busier than the British had realised. The dummies, with their jaunty shakos, achieved their purpose and the British pursuit was delayed. Cavalry then dashed after the French with infantrymen hurrying behind. They found signs of the suffering which the enemy had already endured: starved soldiers lay bloated in the soggy ditches, horses had been slaughtered for meat, and the countryside had been picked clean of all possible provisions.

In the houses [wrote Schaumann], which had to be cleansed by our men before they could be used, dead bodies of French soldiers and animals were found in a state of decomposition . . . A pestilential stench pervaded the deserted streets.

One detachment of hussars had an even more grisly find: they discovered a huge vat of rich red wine, which by some apparent miracle had been left untouched, and they swilled the contents until they neared the bottom – where they found, to their horror, the pickled corpse of a fully-equipped French soldier.

The British had been too late to catch the French before they were firmly positioned; on 24 November Wellington decided no large-scale attempts should be made to dislodge the enemy: he had them cut off from Spain and he believed starvation would force the 50,000 cooped soldiers to surrender. Allied troops settled into winter quarters, still confident. Meanwhile, pressure again mounted for Wellington to take more determined action and fight a battle. He refused, despite slight superiority in numbers, and preferred to wait, writing to William on 8 December:

It is wonderful that they (the French) have been able to remain in the country for so long, and it is scarcely possible that they can remain much longer. If they go, and when they go, their losses will be very great, and mine nothing. If they stay, they must continue to lose men daily, as they do now.

But the French showed no signs of movement during December, and Wellington became increasingly perplexed.

It is certainly astonishing [he reported to Lord Liverpool on the 21st], that the enemy has been able to remain in this country so long . . . With all our money, and having in our favour the good inclinations of the country, I assure you that I could not maintain one division in the district in which they have maintained not less than 60,000 men and 20,000 animals for more than two months.

Wellington suggested one solution to the puzzle – 'they take everything and leave the unfortunate inhabitants to starve.' The British commander was partially correct. Moreover, the scorched earth policy had not been fully carried out: peasants, already

poverty-stricken, had hesitated to destroy all stores and possessions,

The French general
described by Wellington
as the most able he ever
fought, except Napoleon
himself: Marshal André
Masséna. Napoleon
called him 'the favoured
child of victory'. He
came to Spain in May,
1810, surrounded by
glory won in the battles
of Essling and Wagram
against the Austrians.

French forces wind through the Portuguese mountains in September, 1810, as Wellington lures them back to his

prepared defences at Torres Vedras. The French found the route increasingly difficult and dangerous; as Wellington commented:

'There are certainly many bad roads in Portugal, but the enemy had decidedly taken the worst'.

The river Tagus near
Villafranca – southern
end of the British lines
at Torres Vedras.

and had hidden much in caves, walls or underground. By diligence,
torture and murder, the French discovered these hoards. But they
still suffered. More and more men fell from the active list, first
through illness and disease, then from starvation, and always the
Portuguese were ready to pounce upon the unwary.

Despite the increasing horror in the cramped French cantonments and the bloody struggle constantly engaged between French
and Portuguese, the British and French regulars managed to treat
each other with considerable civility during these winter months.
Respective forage parties avoided fighting wherever possible: if
British troops were engaged in forage duties in a particular area
and the French approached, the latter often stood back until the
others had finished and departed. The British obliged in the same
way. On one occasion greyhounds belonging to a British officer
followed a hare into the French lines, and were politely returned.
One night a British sentry came under French fire: next morning
the enemy sent apologies under a flag of truce, saying the man who
had fired had been too panicky. And when in January a British
hussar, Dröse, managed to shoot General Junot through the nose,
Wellington sent an officer to present his condolences and to inquire
after Junot's health. Yet Wellington still searched for the opportunity to slaughter the French, and found it difficult to under-        125

stand why starvation had not accomplished the task for him. But the end fast approached. By February over five hundred Frenchmen were dying each week. Morale and discipline could no longer endure the strain and pain. When Masséna finally began his retreat on the night of 4 March 1811, his army had been seriously reduced: about 50,000 men had filed into the defensive positions in November, now only 46,000 sneaked out, including 11,000 reinforcements who had managed to break through at the beginning of the year. Equally dangerous, Masséna no longer had the confidence of his corps commanders, especially Ney. And now the French had to fight their way back to Spanish safety.

The Torres Vedras system, with the hills dominated by small fortresses, and with British units ready to deploy where most needed.

Wellington also had problems. Reinforcements were expected from England – news of their imminent arrival may have prompted Masséna's breakout – and now he would have to move before they arrived. Many of his best officers were at home on leave, including Hill, Crauford, Leith and Cotton. Moreover, an army under Soult had defeated a Spanish force and now besieged the important border fortress of Badajoz, the southern gateway into Spain. Wellington therefore detached a force under Beresford to move to Elvas, where Soult's advance from Badajoz could be blocked, while the main army hurried after Masséna's bedraggled regiments. At least the British troops could be encouraged by excellent news which soon arrived from Cadiz: General Thomas Graham, commander of the British contingent in

127

the besieged garrison, had launched an attack against Victor's forces and had won a resounding victory on the heights of Barossa. The success boosted Spanish morale, even though the Spanish commander, La Peña, had failed to give Graham adequate support.

Crauford's Light Division, commanded by Sir William Erskine in 'Black Bob's' temporary absence, plunged after the retreating French, together with Pack's Portuguese. Almost immediately the Allies entered a new world of horror, more terrible even than the worst sights so far in the Peninsula. Santarem itself had been reduced to a ghost town, made even more eerie by the melancholy wind-blown booming of a bell in the deserted convent tower. The sound served as apt welcome to the hell in front of the advancing British troops. The countryside, ruined already by the scorched earth policy, had been raked over by the desperate French.

Everything was converted into a wilderness [wrote the omnipresent eye-witness, Schaumann], in which soldiers, vultures, swarms of birds and pigeons grown wild, dogs without masters, wolves and foxes, lived their lives undisturbed. 50,000 of the inhabitants had fled.

Of those who had remained, few survived. One infantryman described the town of Pyrnes, entered on 7 March:

Young women were lying in their houses brutally violated, the streets were strewed with broken furniture, intermixed with putrid carcasses of murdered peasants, mules and donkeys, and every description of filth, that filled the air with pestilential nausea. The few starved male inhabitants who were stalking amid the wreck of their friends and property, looked like so many skeletons who had been permitted to leave their graves for the purpose of taking vengeance.

Badajoz surrendered on 11 March, given up by the treacherous Governor, José Imaz. Soult strutted through the gate and sneered: 'There never was fortress so strong but that a mule load of gold could enter.' Beresford might soon have to face renewed threat from this direction; meanwhile advance units in the main Allied army had been in contact with Masséna's rearguard since 9 March, although the rest of the army were unable to catch up until the morning of the 11th. Nevertheless the French were thrown from Pombal on the 12th before they had had time to blow the bridge over the Soire river; vigorous fighting took place again on the 13th at Redinha but Masséna managed to concentrate his army south of the Mondego. The French commander now had a difficult choice to make: if he could cross the river and force a way through the thin line of Portuguese troops on the north bank he would be in a much safer position, especially if Soult thrust up behind the Allied army. But Wellington's regiments were coming

up fast, and might catch the French in the process of crossing – total destruction would then be almost inevitable. Masséna displayed typical caution and swung east along the southern bank of the Mondego, only just in time. To speed his retreat he ordered all baggage, including ammunition stocks, to be flung away, and all wheeled vehicles except gun carriages were destroyed. Unserviceable animals were hamstrung and left to die, and even the hardened British veterans were sickened when they came across these unfortunate beasts. 'The most disgusting sight,' wrote one British officer, 'was the asses floundering in the mud, some with throats half cut, the rest barbarously houghed.' Wellington's army had to make a short halt while food was brought up on the 16th. Pursuit continued next dawn. Everywhere the advancing British saw horrors perpetrated by the enemy: the remains of women and children strung from trees, with fires still smouldering beneath their charred swinging feet; horribly mutilated bodies; ruined homes and polluted streams. In one village street shocked British soldiers found the crushed body of a woman: she had been laid on her back, alive, with a huge rock on her breasts– four British soldiers were needed to shift it.

By 20 March, the birthday of Napoleon's son, the King of Rome, Wellington felt sufficiently confident to send troop transports

Part of the French defensive area at Santarem, carefully planned by Masséna – but the scene of terrible French suffering.

home from Lisbon. Two days later Wellington's optimism further increased: the British commander received reports that Masséna, now at Celorico, had started a move south-east to Guarda instead of east to Almeida as expected. This new route, via Castelo Branco, would cross far more difficult terrain, with even less chance of supplies. Ney disagreed with this change of direction, probably undertaken to avoid the humiliation of retreating over the same road the French army had used in the advance, and was immediately dismissed from his corps command. By 29 March, after further hardships along the more difficult route, Masséna was forced to change his mind and retreat due east again; the mistake had cost valuable time, and Reynier's corps barely managed to avoid defeat at Sabugal in the Coa valley on 3 April. But now

General Thomas Graham leads his troops from besieged Cadiz to inflict heavy defeat on the French on the Barossa heights.

Masséna scuttled into Spain and managed to reach his Salamanca base on 11 April. The day before, Wellington had issued a coolly triumphant proclamation:

The Portuguese are informed that the cruel enemy . . . have been obliged to evacuate, after suffering great losses, and have retired across the Agueda. The inhabitants of the country are therefore at liberty to return to their homes.

Masséna had made only two serious mistakes during the Portugal campaign: the decision to take the initial north road to Coimbra, and the foolish move towards Castelo Branco; otherwise his tactics and strategy had been extremely skilful. He had managed to extricate his army from threatened annihilation. But if Masséna displayed skill, Wellington showed brilliance. Masséna, for all his cunning, had lost between 25,000 and 30,000 men – over thirty-eight per cent of his total army, plus immense quantities of guns and valuable equipment. Psychologically, the loss was even greater. The fourth of March 1811, the day Masséna started his retreat from Portugal, marked a turning point in the whole Napoleonic War. Masséna started the French on the road to final defeat, a road which would lead from this far hot corner of Europe via burning Moscow and the freezing Beresina in 1812, through blazing Leipzig in 1813 to the occupation of Paris and the abdication of the all-powerful Napoleon Bonaparte.

'The war is now likely to take on a new shape,' confided Wellington. The British could now move onto the offensive, and, if the French obliged, could plunge into pitched battle. Almeida had become the only point in Portugal in enemy hands, and provisions for the garrison were known to be short; Wellington ordered forces to keep the fortress isolated as a bait for a French relief attempt. The Allied army remained split between the section under his direct control in the north and the forces commanded by Beresford further south; on 16 April Wellington rode off to confer with the latter, inspected the situation over the border at Badajoz, and ordered this French-held fortress to be re-invested. He allowed Beresford considerable powers of discretion, including permission to fight a battle if he thought fit. Wellington then made all haste back to the main army, arriving during the evening of the 28th: at any moment the reinforced French could advance to support Almeida and battle might be joined. And only four days later Masséna crossed the Agueda at Ciudad Rodrigo with over 45,000 men.

Wellington had only about 37,500 troops, but they included his most experienced veterans, all of them supremely confident; and the French could only manage to drag thirty-eight guns with them to match the Allies' forty-eight. The French advanced rapidly, but Wellington had already selected the battle site, and carefully deployed his forces during 2 May between the parallel Turones and Dos Casas rivers, tributaries of the Douro. The main road from Ciudad Rodrigo crossed the Dos Casas into Portugal at the village of Fuentes de Onoro, with narrow streets climbing the steep hillside to a boulder-littered plateau stretching back two miles to the Turones. North of the village the Dos Casas roared through a deep gorge extending up to Fort Concepcion east of Almeida. South-

wards the river split into a number of smaller streams. An enemy advance either north or south of the village would therefore be difficult: Wellington hoped the French would have to move straight upon Fuentes de Onoro, and he therefore positioned the bulk of his army in and behind the houses, with two divisions, the 6th and 5th, extending northwards towards Fort Concepcion. Early on 3 May Wellington watched the French deploy for attack. He could see a force of approximately three divisions moving north towards Fort Concepcion – these would have difficulty crossing the river and would then be met by the 5th and 6th divisions. The main enemy strength seemed about to advance direct against the village: Masséna would therefore oblige Wellington with a frontal assault. And, at 2 pm, the longest battle of the Peninsular War began.

Masséna was determined to avenge the humiliation Wellington had heaped upon him during the last dreadful months in Portugal. So too were his men. And no less than ten battalions now marched against Fuentes de Onoro. Allied skirmishers hidden behind the walls and buildings on the west bank took the full force. Bullets swept over the water; the French line lapped the far bank and hundreds of men began to splash knee-deep through the river; scores of them fell, but more came on holding muskets high as they waded towards the British bank. Some reached the Allied lines and

The siege of Badajoz, 1811, after Wellington had ordered Beresford to re-invest the city.

133

defenders stood from cover to lunge with their bayonets. A French foothold was gained, but Allied reinforcements were sent running through the alley-ways and the French were driven back again. Already humped bodies of the enemy studded the river like sodden blue stepping-stones. The French could be seen rallying and re-forming ranks, and the defenders hurriedly prepared themselves for the next assault. 'They're coming. See them coming!' And on they came, some of them running in their haste to reach the west bank and to escape from the humming crescendo of musket fire into hand-to-hand fighting. Over 4,000 French splashed through the water, and they seemed to the defenders like a thick, unstoppable mass; up they climbed along the west bank, jumping over walls, forcing their way into the streets in a jumble of shouting, shooting, blue and grey uniforms, and the Allies were pushed back, yard by yard, building to building. Cobbles were covered with dripping corpses and still the French came on. The village was lost, with British and Portuguese troops running, firing, running again, up to the ridge beyond. Wellington ordered two more regiments into the attack, supported by a third. Down they went into the smoking stinking streets. The village swayed back into Allied hands and some troops even crossed the river to fight on the far side, and as darkness fell Fuentes remained under Wellington's control.

Foggy dawn arrived on 4 May with Wellington's troops anxiously standing ready for the expected assault. They peered forward into the mist rising from the river; but no serious attack came. Skirmishing fire died down by about 10 am and a tacit truce continued for the rest of the day when Allies and French joined in the grisly task of prising the stiffening corpses from the jammed alley-ways in the village. So thick were the bodies that those buried deep underneath were still warm and soft. Enemies worked together and passed one another with averted eyes, not through hostility, but as if ashamed of the atrocity which they had committed and which they knew would soon start again. During the afternoon enemy cavalry movements could be seen to the south of the French line, and it seemed preparations were being made to turn the Allied flank by an advance across the stream network below the village. Nothing developed that day, but Wellington made plans to deal with such a threat.

This came early on the 5th under cover of swirling mist. About 3,500 cavalry and three infantry divisions managed to cross the main Dos Casas river and the two tributaries to the west, then took the village of Nave de Haver from surprised Portuguese troops, before forcing back British cavalry to the hamlet of Poco Vehlo further north. Reinforcements failed to restore the situation; at the same time Masséna launched another assault direct upon Fuentes. The position became critical; even the unflappable Wellington admitted: 'We must mind a little what we are about.' To the south the 7th division was in danger of complete annihilation from massed French cavalry and several batteries of mobile artillery. Crauford, who had returned from leave only the evening before, was ordered to take his Light Division to support the 7th: Wellington stipulated that Crauford should bring the 7th back northwards and should not attempt to maintain a line further south – this would have caused the centre of the Allied army to shift too far away from covering Almeida; on the other hand, by allowing the French to have possession of this flanking area, Allied communications back into Portugal through Guarda would be severed. Wellington staked all upon ultimate victory.

Crauford substituted his own division for the 7th and then carried out a masterly, text-book withdrawal which drew gasps of admiration from watching staff officers – both British and French. Packs of French cavalry and three infantry divisions plus mobile artillery all swarmed around the heavily outnumbered Light Division. If the cavalry were allowed to pin down the British to enable infantry and artillery to concentrate upon them, terrible and total destruction of the division would have been inevitable. No further troops could be spared for reinforcements. Yet Crauford's division and Cotton's cavalry now proceeded to manoeuvre as if on parade. The few British horsemen kept the artillery at bay, charging again and again wherever the enemy tried to line their guns, until horses were almost on their knees with weariness and riders had to drag on the reins to hold up their animals' heads. Crauford had ordered his line battalions to withdraw in mobile squares, each battalion moving alternately, and with riflemen outside these tight formations acting as skirmishers. Square by square, the men withdrew in steady, orderly moves amongst the battle confusion smoking around them. With superb self-control and discipline and with 'Black Bob's' commands ringing clear above the thundering guns and snapping muskets, the division retired two terrible miles. Enemy cavalry charges broke against the squares like huge waves. Six guns of Bull's horse artillery gave brave support, sometimes staying until the enemy almost enveloped them: one pair, commanded by Captain Norman Ramsay, became totally engulfed by massed blue uniforms, and were given up for lost; but Ramsay ordered his pieces to be limbered up, his gunners leapt upon horses with sabres drawn, and they hacked and

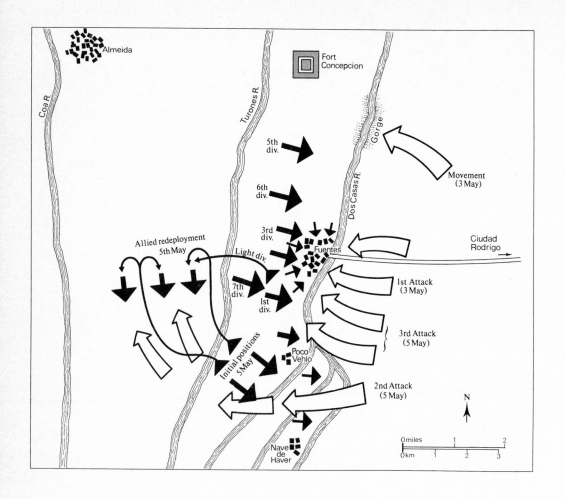

Map 4  The Battle of Fuentes de Onoro, May 1811.

pushed their way through again. And the Light Division joined the reformed British line. In front gathered a force of 22,000 French awaiting the order to attack.

But Masséna knew that to launch this southern assault before the village of Fuentes had been taken in the centre would be to risk having his army sliced in two. Fuentes therefore remained the key, and fighting in the blood-swilling streets now reached a monstrous climax. Ten battalions were driving over the river and into the houses; Highland troops were forced back, then pushed forward again. Back came the French; more Allied reinforcements plunged in; once more the French were thrown out. And now Masséna ordered an assault by eighteen battalions – probably two whole divisions. No defence could withstand this terrible pounding and the gore-glutted alleys were taken again, with the French forcing on, up the slopes to the ridge – only to be met by the advancing Connaught Rangers and Mackinnon's brigade and hurled back into the village again. Scottish Highlanders rallied and staggered back into the battle, and neither side could be prised from its grip upon the choking streets and battered buildings: the whole village became a holocaust of vomiting muskets, stabbing bayonets, violent explosions, shrieking struggling soldiers. Yard by yard the Scots and Irishmen punched their way over the corpses and reached the river; over the red and greasy water went the grappling men and on to the French bank. The village had been pulled back into Allied control – and would remain so; the French massed for another attack but failed to carry it forward. An artillery duel to the west subsided; Wellington remained master of the field, and ordered his troops to dig in during the night of the 5th.

By 6 May Masséna realised any further attempt to force a victory would be useless, and contented himself with manoeuvring his cavalry. 'They looked uncommonly well,' wrote Kincaid, a rifleman in Crauford's division, 'and we were proud to think that we had beaten such fine-looking fellows.' A few days later Wellington described the Battle of Fuentes de Onoro as 'the most difficult one I was ever concerned in, and against the greatest odds . . . If Boney had been there, we should have been beaten.' Wellington had insufficient strength, especially in cavalry, to attempt a counter-attack; Masséna on the other hand could not accomplish his task of relieving Almeida, and instead sent through a message to the garrison instructing the governor to blow up the place and attempt an escape. The French had lost 2,192 men to the Allied 1,545 – most of these within a tiny patch of ground now covered by the smoking, stinking ruins of Fuentes. The French withdrew very early on the 10th; Wellington expressed no surprise: 'I thought they meant to be off.' But Masséna had the last word: acting under his instructions the Almeida garrison blew up the fortress and escaped, with their daring bid for safety helped by the incompetence of a number of British officers, one of whom afterwards blew out his brains.

Meanwhile General Sir William Beresford had besieged Badajoz on 5 May. Hopes were high for an early collapse: provisions were known to be low and defensive fortifications incomplete. But on 12 May reports reached Beresford of a speech made by Soult at Seville on the 8th, when the French marshal had boasted he would lead a strong force to relieve the garrison. Within twenty-four hours contact had been made with the approaching French: Soult's forces were divided into two columns, one heading from

Seville under Soult himself, the other coming in from the east under La Tour-Maubourg. Total enemy strength would be about 25,000; Beresford had an Anglo-Portuguese army of 20,310, plus the use of two Spanish armies under Blake and Castaños. The British general broke off the Badajoz siege, and aimed to stop Soult far enough south to prevent reinforcements reaching the garrison; by 2 pm on the 15th the Allied army had reached Albuera, a small town on the west bank of the river of the same name, and here the battle would be fought. A number of similarities exist between the clash at Albuera and that just finished at Fuentes de Onoro: on both occasions the French marched to relieve a besieged garrison and the Allies attempted to block this advance by defending a main river crossing, with the key to the battle resting in the small town, or village, at the centre. But important differences were also evident: the Allies at Albuera outnumbered the enemy, unlike the situation at Fuentes, and yet the army at the latter battle had been commanded by Wellington; now, although the Duke was galloping towards the scene of action, he would arrive too late to control the fighting. Victory or defeat lay in Beresford's hands.

The main Anglo-Portuguese army hurriedly deployed in and behind Albuera, with a Portuguese division and brigade to the north and with the southern flank protected by Blake's Spanish army which arrived late on the 15th. About 4,000 French infantry, 550 cavalry and twelve guns comprised the first enemy attack, launched at 8 am on the 16th and striking direct at Albuera although moving to the north of the main road. At the same time an even stronger force appeared just south of this road, opposite Blake's Spanish army. Beresford's expectation of a frontal assault seemed correct. But then came an alarming development: French cavalry suddenly appeared much further south, already across the two small tributaries of the Albuera river and heading towards the flank of the Spanish army situated on the extreme Allied right. Spanish cavalry were routed. And now nineteen battalions of French infantry emerged from thick trees in this sector, formed up into columns and prepared to roll up the Spanish army. Blake received urgent orders: the Spanish army must reform into line facing south to meet this threat; hurrying south in support were troops of the British 2nd division. Blake, mistakenly believing the main attack would still come across the brooks to the east, where the first French troops to advance were still massed, only redeployed a quarter of his force – amounting to a mere four battalions. Against this slender line Soult now threw 8,400 men spreading across four hundred yards and protected by 3,500

cavalry. A dozen drums beat out a deadly, blood-chilling tattoo as the enemy host advanced; only the slender three-man-deep Spanish line stood to defend the entire flank of the Allied army. But the Spaniards now fought with terrible bravery: increasing gaps torn in the stretched line were filled by men from the two ranks behind, and the 2nd division came up on the right flank to give support, and incredibly the French were checked.

Few men had noticed the sullen storm-clouds looming on the horizon, and thunder rumbles had been drowned by the guns. But now a violent downpour swept across the field; sheets of rain drenched the sweating men and their muskets – and the latter, requiring dry priming, could no longer be fired. Enemy cavalry, mainly Polish lancers, sliced in to take advantage. Colborne's brigade, the leading brigade in the 2nd division, received the full impact of this attack and three battalions were annihilated in as many minutes before they had time to form squares. Cavalry carved onwards, through the lines and into the rear, and Beresford barely managed to save himself by thrusting aside a Polish lance and throwing the enemy rider from his horse. On went the cavalry against Allied artillery and against British reinforcements

139

Beresford fends off an attack by a Polish lancer during the enemy cavalry charge at the Battle of Albuera.

hurrying up to the front. The Spanish line had now lost thirty per cent of its original strength and some units were wavering under the cavalry attack; Beresford ordered them replaced by seven British battalions. Rain ceased as suddenly as it had begun, and these 3,700 Allied troops could now use their muskets: but they remained opposed by the bulk of two French divisions, still totalling about 7,800 men. And the resulting close-range fire fight was probably the most ferocious in all military history. Carnage continued for almost an hour, in a packed two acres of bloody mud: men battered each other with musket butts and bare hands, they stabbed and clawed, they fired one spewing volley after another until they could hardly raise their arms and their shoulders were bleeding raw from the recoils; they could see no further than a few yards in the choking smoke, and all they could see in that short space were bodies, limbs, and sweating, staring, frenzied faces. Firing dwindled as men ran out of ammunition, but still they fought, clambering over corpses to reach out at one another, swaying and struggling upon the dead and dying. Nearly four-fifths of Hoghton's brigade were down and Hoghton himself had been slain; the severely wounded colonel of one regiment lay where he had fallen and refused to be moved, crying out: 'Die hard 57th! Die hard!' And his men obeyed. Beresford became almost berserk trying to find reinforcements: Carlos de España's Spanish brigade was ordered into the fight but would not advance into effective range, and Beresford grabbed one of its colonels and dragged him bodily towards the fearsome struggle, hoping the rest of the men would follow, but still they refused. Instructions to Hamilton, deployed further north, failed to arrive. Meanwhile Lowry Cole had decided on his own initiative to throw his 4th division into the attack on the right of the dreadful conflict; his men advanced in a long line from behind Albuera, and immediately met French counter-attacks consisting mainly of cavalry, directed to the west of his line, and soon followed by 5,600 infantrymen plus close artillery support. Forces clashed and locked together, swaying backwards and forwards in an awesome stranglehold and shrouded by thickening smoke. The French broke first. Retreat began with individual soldiers, then groups, then whole units; others wavered and Portuguese troops were thrown in to push the retreat into rout. Back over the brooks poured the remnants of the proud French battalions. Torrential rain swept over the battlefield again, to drown the dying in the mud and to sluice the blood from thousands of ghastly wounds.

It is impossible [declared Beresford], by any description to do justice to the distinguished gallantry of the troops; but every individual nobly did his duty; and it is observed that our dead, particularly the 57th Regiment, were lying as they fought, in ranks, and every wound was in the front.

This moving tribute from the normally ineloquent Sir William made a fitting epitaph to the 5,916 Allies who were slain, 4,159 of them British. These casualties were mainly confined to comparatively few units: regiments in the thick of the fighting, totalling 8,738 men, lost 4,039 dead and wounded, and three of the four British brigades had insufficient survivors to see to their fallen comrades. But the French suffered worst – about 8,000 men were slaughtered – and the following day, 17 May, Soult began to withdraw along the road by which he had come.

Beresford resumed the siege of Badajoz on 19 May and Wellington marched reinforcements south to replace the Albuera casualties. He remained to command this southern force, leaving Brent Spencer in charge in the north. Now began weeks of anxious manoeuvring. Early in June, reports indicated Soult was about to march for Badajoz again, and at the same time Spencer be-

French troops capture
Tarragona, June
1811 – one of the reasons
for Wellington's decision
to withdraw across the
Guadiana.

lieved Marmont might be moving west towards him. Badajoz
had therefore to be reduced in minimum time if the Allies were to
avoid being trapped. The first assault on the fortress, launched on
6 June, failed to make a breach, and Wellington wrote to Stuart
on the 8th: 'Badajoz may fall, but the business will be very near run
on both sides.' Another assault on the 9th failed to crack the thick
defences. Spencer's apprehension meanwhile increased and despite
reassurances from Wellington he insisted on destroying supplies and
moving south; by 13 June his force had been deployed within a
day's march of Badajoz. By now French defences were beginning
to crumble, but Wellington had also heard that 60,000 enemy
troops might soon be marching against his 44,000. And on
17 June Wellington began to withdraw across the Guadiana; next
day Marmont and Soult joined forces at Merida and entered
Badajoz on the 20th – the day on which the garrison ran out of
food. French probes were launched against the Allied positions
on 22 June, but the enemy hesitated to undertake full-scale attack.

I have all the French troops in Spain in my front [wrote Wellington on the
26th]. They have been looking at us for a week and the more they look
at us the less they like us and I believe that I should get over the crisis at
the moment without a battle, of which we can at present ill spare the
necessary loss, however confident I am of the result.

Within twenty-four hours Wellington's scouts reported the movement of French forces withdrawing to the south-east. It seemed a
battle was to be avoided for the moment. And on the 29th Soult
began to move off in the direction of Seville, leaving Marmont on

the Guadiana with 47,000 men. Wellington's army remained un-molested and at rest. To start with, the British relished the inactivity. Rifleman Kincaid wrote:

Up to this period it had been a matter of no small difficulty to ascertain, at any time, the day of the week; that of the month was altogether out of the question, and could only be reckoned by counting back to the date of the last battle; but our division was here joined by a chaplain, whose duty it was to remind us of these things.

Men whiled away the time by cockfighting, flea-hunting and scorpion-baiting. But within a few days disease began to creep in amongst the troops. The cantonments were impossible to keep clean; wounds festered; rats scurried everywhere to spread the filth. Plague broke out and hundreds of men went sick, and the dead mounted. Marmont, also suffering, withdrew his army north and east on 15 July.

Plentiful supplies had now been piled in Badajoz and the fortress would be extremely difficult to take; Wellington decided instead to leave the citadel for the moment and to concentrate on Ciudad Rodrigo. The latter fortress was blockaded in August, but no siege operations could be started for the time being. Allied forces moved into cantonments along the communica-tion routes between the northern and southern corridors into Spain, with Wellington moving north early in August to establish his HQ at Fuenteguinaldo. Hill took over the southern command. Almost immediately a new threat developed: on 23 August Mar-mont joined forces with Dorsenne, now commander of the French army of the north. Intelligence reports gave enemy manpower strength as about 60,000, while Wellington's army numbered only 46,000. But on 27 August Wellington still gave a hopeful, although cautious, opinion to Lord Liverpool, that the war had become 'to a certain degree offensive on our part,' and at a dinner on the 29th he commented that from the reports of the great magazines forming on the frontier he believed Bonaparte in person was coming to command the French, adding: 'I am damned if he will drive us out.' Within a few days this optimism had faded. Marmont drove forward and forced the British to lift the blockade of Ciudad Rodrigo, and Wellington's army was almost caught off-balance between 25 and 28 September as it retired south-west towards the mountains behind the Coa. Wellington himself barely managed to avoid capture on the 25th. Marmont withdrew from Ciudad Rodrigo again. For the moment campaigning was over: on 1 October 1811, the Allies thankfully retired into canton-ments for three months' rest.

Chapter 7

# Advance –
# and Retire

'**D**addy' Hill's men still had serious work to do before they could settle for the winter. On 22 October the southern commander suddenly stabbed into Spain south of the Tagus and took Gerard's force of 2,500 unawares at Arroyo Molinos. British troops charged into the unprepared enemy accompanied by rolling thunder and howling wind, and, on 4 November, Hill returned in triumph with over 1,300 prisoners. About 800 of the enemy had been left dead or wounded, and the Allies had only lost just over 100 men.

Meanwhile British soldiers in cantonments were enjoying such pleasures as they could find in the barren, chilly landscape around them. At least the colder weather cured summer sicknesses. Officers improvised ambitious horse races: these entailed travelling in an absolutely straight line from point A to point B, regardless of obstacles, and much merriment resulted from the sight of gallant officers trying to drag unwilling mounts over the roof of a peasant's hovel. Hunting became a favourite pastime, and as always the men sought out local feminine company. Kincaid recalled:

We invited the villagers, every evening, to a dance at our quarters . . . A Spanish peasant girl has an address about her which I have never met with in the same class of any other country . . . We used to flourish away at the bolero, fandango and waltz, and wound up early in the evening with a supper of roasted chestnuts.

Even this began to pall after many days of the same diet.

We found that the cherry cheek and sparkling eye of rustic beauty furnished but a very poor apology for the illuminated portion of Nature's fairest works, and ardently longed for an opportunity of once more feasting our eyes on a *lady*.

The bloody fields of Fuentes and Albuera nevertheless seemed far away.

But not for long. Barely had Christmas celebrations closed when Wellington heard that Suchet's army was about to be reinforced for use in Valencia, and these extra men, totalling 15,000, would be taken from Marmont's army opposite the Allied lines in the north. Wellington immediately seized the opportunity. The twin fortresses of Ciudad Rodrigo and Badajoz still guarded the north and south gateways to Spain, through which the Allies must pass: on 8 January 1812, Wellington's army therefore suddenly advanced to surround the former. The first troops made rapid time over the frost-hard ground and reached Ciudad Rodrigo by early afternoon:

*Opposite* The first foothold is gained on the smoking Badajoz walls: soon the city will be sacked by punch-drunk British troops.

145

French officers, seeing the small number of attackers, came out of the gate and bowed in ridicule. The Allies had no time for pleasantries: within a few days Marmont could counter-attack. Night fell early on the 8th, and Colonel Colborne of the 52nd crept forward with ten volunteer companies towards the hill known as the Great Teson, upon which the French had placed an important redoubt. The attackers reached within fifty yards of the defences before being discovered, then one group kept up continuous fire to keep French heads down while the other six companies swarmed in. The place fell within twenty minutes. And now the Allies began to dig towards the fortress itself, making good progress in the winter-firm soil. Allied batteries began firing at 4.30 pm on the 13th and the French were forced in from the suburbs. Further trenches were dug under cover of thick fog on the 16th; artillery fire intensified next day, and two breaches had been battered in the walls by the 19th. Wellington sat down to write the crucial order: 'The attack of Ciudad Rodrigo must be made this evening at 7 o'clock.'

First troops, commanded by Colonel O'Toole, struck ten minutes early. The bridge over the Agueda on the opposite side of the fortress soon fell into Allied hands, together with a French outpost and two guns. Campbell's brigade filtered past this outpost, broke into the ditch before the main ramparts, and raced along to the main breach to join other assaulting troops. These two brigades began to clamber up the breach, only to find when they reached the summit that a sixteen-foot ditch had been newly dug between this outer wall and the next line of defences. While they attempted to find a way across, the men came under heavy fire from muskets, howitzers and grenades, but the gap was bridged and survivors swarmed on. More redcoats began to jump and scramble into the fortress; then a massive explosion rent the night air, sending up huge sparks and vivid red and yellow flames: the French had planted a colossal mine under the breach, ready to be blown in an emergency. Meanwhile the Light Division streamed into the second breach; Allied troops were fanning out through the bullet-sprayed streets. More men flooded over the walls, despite vicious grapeshot and whistling shells. The French garrison retreated further into the town with the Allies hard after them. Sparks stitched the black night; men blundered into one another and slaughtered friends in error; bayonets stabbed into shadows; grenades were lobbed through house windows. Within two hours Ciudad Rodrigo had been taken, but the victorious troops were now in an almost un-

controllable frenzy: buildings blazed, rooms were ripped apart,

General 'Daddy' Hill, quiet-spoken and gentle, yet capable of brilliant audacity: a leader who took trouble to see to the well-being of his men.

men rushed everywhere, shouting and screaming. Soon they discovered wine, and drunkenness increased the disorder: men shot each other and their officers, some soldiers drowned themselves in brandy casks and wine vats, while others simply sat and sobbed. Order was gradually and ruthlessly restored in the last hours before dawn, with some officers risking their lives in doing so: General Picton was especially evident, lashing out at marauding soldiers with a smashed musket barrel.

The Allies lost 568 men storming Ciudad Rodrigo and the French about the same. One British fatality caused special pain:

Wine cooler, part of the Prussian Service at the Wellington Museum, illustrating the blowing up of the huge French mine during the storming of Ciudad Rodrigo.

'Black Bob' Crauford, the fiery and brilliant commander of the Light Division, the man whose waspish tongue, black temper and harsh disciplinary methods had been famous and feared throughout the army, who had trained his troops to campaign and fight without regard to comfort or convenience. Crauford had been well known for his insistence that formations must never break ranks or even step when marching, regardless of obstacles, and if a soldier stepped over a puddle instead of striding through it he had risked a mighty bellow: 'Sit down in it, Sir, sit down!' Now the Light Division buried their leader, and found their own way to pay respects – marching away from the fresh grave they came to a body-clogged ice-skimmed pool, fifty yards across, and instead of taking the track around the edge they plunged on in silence, officers and men almost up to their waists in the foul and freezing water.

Badajoz remained to be attended to. Hurried orders were sent south for preparations to be made; the main army marched in mid-February; Wellington himself, leaving his departure as long as possible to deceive the French, began his journey on 6 March, to arrive five days later. Once again speed was essential: Badajoz had to be taken before the French could re-possess Ciudad Rodrigo. The fortress was invested on 16 March and the first parallel dug next day amidst violent thunder-storms; both British and French sweated in the rain to carve out muddy trenches, with the enemy attempting to impede the Allied advance by flanking fire. The French sallied out on the 19th; the Allies retaliated on the 22nd by taking San Christobal on the other side of the Guadiana river from Badajoz itself. Two days later the Allies made a major, although painful, gain by the capture of Fort Picurina in the south-east area of the city and additional guns opened up on the French garrison. But on the 29th Wellington received news from the north: Marmont's army had been reported marching towards Ciudad Rodrigo. Time was running out, yet the French still showed no signs of weakness at Badajoz. Wellington's time-schedule had started to suffer. On 6 April, Easter Sunday, he was told three breaches had been made: none of them were large and the enemy behind them were extremely strong. Wellington knew full well an attack would result in terrible slaughter. He gave orders for an assault to start at 7.30 pm, hesitated, then ordered the attack to be launched at 10 pm. Five thrusts would be made: the Light and 4th divisions would storm two of the breaches, leaving the third un-touched; Picton's 3rd division would attack the castle in the north-east; Leith's 5th division would attempt to scale the walls in the north-west; 1,000 men under Major Wilson would strike at the Lunette San Roche positions in the east.

Just before the allotted hour a sullen stillness spread over the city. Men murmured in their trenches, drained canteens to slake parched mouths, sat on their packs and waited, or handed final messages to comrades to be passed to wives or mothers. The Light and 4th divisions advanced into the brooding silence towards the breaches. As the thick deep columns crept forward, leading British soldiers could hear French guards talking as they paced the ramparts above; clouds scudded across the night sky beyond. Redcoats lined the forward trenches ready for the dash to the walls, but just before 10 pm an enemy sentry by the left breach heard a chink in the darkness to his front, perhaps the scrape of bayonet against stone. '*Qui vive? Qui vive?*' he called and receiving no reply he fired his musket into the black. The crack cut the death-like silence and almost before the sharp echo died the British soldiers heard the abrupt beating of a French drum-roll, urging the garrison to arms. The roll ended, and silence came again even deeper than before. Ten long minutes remained till 10 o'clock and the time for attack. And then the British by the breach heard shouts and firing, and sudden explosions, from the opposite side of Badajoz in the castle area, where Picton's men were meant to be scaling the walls. This assault had been discovered before time: the French, suspecting an attempt, had thrown the lighted corpse of a British soldier from the high walls to illuminate the ground around, and this ghoulish torch had enabled the defenders to see Picton's 3rd division waiting in the flickering shadows.

The Light and 4th divisions by the breach struck now, while the tumult by the castle still sounded – but the waiting French replied with a tremendous volley to shatter the British ranks even before they advanced ten yards from their cover trenches; then survivors found that ditches in front of them had filled with water and horrible mud, or had been sown with small mines by the resourceful French. More men fell, to drown in the mire, or were blown apart by the mines and howitzer fire; but still more men were pushing from behind, and on they went into the raging inferno and earth-trembling din of bursting shells and grenades, roaring guns from the flanks, crashing iron howitzers, heavy rolls and cracklings from powder-barrels, and everywhere zipping blazing splinters of chipped rock and shredded wood. In front lay the gap blown into the ramparts which Wellington knew to be insufficiently large, and now, in Napier's words: 'The breach, which, yawning and glittering with steel, seemed like the mouth of a huge dragon, belching forth smoke and flames.' The British columns pushed and clawed up the rubble only to find the French had more horrors for them.

Across the top [wrote one sergeant], glittered a range of sword-blades, sharp-pointed, keen-edged on both sides, and firmly fixed in ponderous beams, which were chained together and set deep in the ruins; and for ten feet in front the ascent was covered with loose planks studded with sharp iron points, on which the feet of the foremost being set, the planks moved.

Soldiers slid screaming with the pain of the spikes in their feet, down on to those coming up behind. The French just beyond kept up terrific fire at almost point-blank range – each defender had a number of prepared muskets by him, and as well as normal bullets the British suffered a type of spraying buck-shot. A solid mass of men jammed below the breach, shoving and jostling, and those in front were pushed bodily onto the deadly sword-blade fence at the summit; others tried to crawl over their writhing bodies, only to be thrown back again. Jeering Frenchmen shouted down: '*Entrez! Entrez!* Why don't you come into Badajoz?' For two hours the hellish carnage continued. Reports of the fighting were fed to Wellington and his sun-burnt face turned yellow as he read the ghastly details.

Picton's men were storming the castle walls, deemed to be the most unlikely section for a successful assault. Men ran forward carrying swaying ladders which were thrown up against the black, glistening stones. Up swarmed the troops, ripped by flank fire and bombarded by a deluge of rocks, logs, and bursting shells rolled off the parapet. Pikes and bayonets were thrust into the faces of those

Badajoz inferno: massed British troops push towards the terrible French sword barrier; in the foreground are the flooded trenches.

151

who reached the topmost rungs; ladders were thrown from the walls; the British pulled back. Leith's 5th division, an hour late in starting its attack at the north-west corner of the town, met with similar failure. But Picton's and Leith's troops tried again. More ladders were rushed forward, the men stumbling over the crushed remains of those who had fallen. Up climbed the men, to be thrown, stabbed, and shot down again. 'It was almost impossible to twinkle an eye on any man before he was knocked down,' exclaimed one participant. But ladders continually clattered onto the walls and within seconds were thick with clinging men; and then troops waiting their turn saw a solitary redcoat on the rampart struggling with the French. 'Up! Up! One man up!' And then another. Cheers burst from the struggling men. Three out of every four soldiers who crawled over the top were hacked down again but survivors grew in number and strength, and the French were forced back over the bodies; a bloody finger-hold had been gained. Picton's and Leith's divisions forced forward at the north-west and north-east corners. Picton himself fell wounded, but his men went on. The time was about midnight. The French commander, Phillipon, had to rush more men into these corners to bolster the defence, so weakening strength at the southern breaches. In the early hours of the 7th Allied troops were flooding in from all quarters, and the French pulled back across the river to San Christobal where Phillipon would be obliged to surrender later that morning.

Allied troops advanced cautiously into the inner town and found the lamp-lit streets incredibly quiet – a silence even more remarkable in contrast to the hell just behind them. But the troops brought this hell with them. They had a blood-lust; they were stupefied by fear and frenzy; they were further incensed by occasional shots fired now from beneath the houses by pro-French Spaniards. And the men became completely crazed: Wellington's army had become a tortured, pain-maddened animal. Badajoz suffered a sacking which made the treatment of Ciudad Rodrigo seem almost civilised. For almost forty-eight hours the troops ran amok, and because their officers were unable – or unwilling – to control their men, the terrible behaviour constituted the worst mutiny in the history of the British army. As one captain reported:

The infuriated soldiery resembled rather a pack of hell-hounds vomited up from the infernal regions for the extirpation of mankind than what they were twelve short hours previously – a well-organised, brave, disciplined and obedient British army, and burning only with impatience for what is called glory.

Riots began to break out with a sullen, swelling roar of shouting soldiers, splintering wood, fierce crackling flames and shattering shots. Drink quickly affected men already swaying with weariness, and they staggered about the streets to collapse in the gutters with liquid bubbling from their open mouths. Houses were ripped apart in search of loot; churches were plundered and wine-sodden soldiers caroused in the aisles and stood upon the altars shouting obscenities. Men dragged screaming civilians into the streets and clubbed them to death. Crawling babies were shot and bayoneted for sport. Whimpering women and young girls had their clothes ripped from them and were flung naked in the mud, and blood-stained soldiers took their sweating pleasure in turns. Nuns ran screeching through the rubble, clawing to find a hole in which to hide. Daylight on the 7th merely made the scene more horrible and riots and rape only subsided when men became too exhausted or satiated to stir themselves. Wellington issued a rather pathetic order: 'It is full time that the plunder of Badajoz should cease.' The British commander was in fact filled with terrible weariness and grief, more so than at any other time in the campaign: he had visited the ramparts and had seen the mounds of corpses and his stern face, normally so calm and controlled, had been streaked with tears. He wrote a sad dispatch to Lord Liverpool:

The capture of Badajoz affords as strong an instance of the gallantry of our troops as has ever been displayed. But I greatly hope that I shall never again be the instrument of putting them to such a test.

About 4,760 casualties had been suffered, with the Light and 4th divisions losing 2,500 men in a few yards at the breaches in just two hours. The French garrison had totalled only 5,003; only a handful escaped the battle and the terrible behaviour of Allied troops immediately afterwards.

Those few French survivors took the news to Soult in the south and Marmont in the centre: Wellington had grabbed the keys of Spain. Marmont entered Castelo Branco on 12 April, but retreated immediately he learnt of the fall of Badajoz. Wellington had achieved astonishing success: his army had been outnumbered three to one, with the enemy thrusting against him in both north and south, yet he had managed to manoeuvre not only to avoid being trapped, but to smash open the two gateways in turn – Ciudad Rodrigo in twelve days and Badajoz in twenty. And soon the Allied advance could begin.

But success failed to change Wellington's cool, methodical attitude: preparations must be made. Communications were improved back to Lisbon and Oporto; on 12 May a preliminary sortie was undertaken by Hill, advancing from Merida against the French positions on the Tagus at Almarez, and as a result direct links between Soult and Marmont were severed. Also Wellington had two extra factors in his favour for the forthcoming advance into Spain. The first involved changes now being made to French forces in Spain, largely as a result of Napoleon's determination to launch the Grand Army against recalcitrant Russia: many of the best French units were being replaced, including Polish battalions and lancers and the Imperial Guard, and French armies in Spain were reduced to five. Suchet commanded 60,000 men in Valencia; in central Spain Marmont had his 52,000-strong Army of Portugal and Dorsenne had his Army of the North, 48,000; Soult's Army of the South, in Andalusia, totalled 54,000, while a further 18,500 men remained in and around Madrid under Joseph Bonaparte – overall commander in Spain. This gave a French grand total of over 230,000 men. Wellington had only 60,000. But to help balance this numerical discrepancy came the second favourable factor. Wellington's victories and growing resentment against the French stimulated increased guerrilla warfare, which played an essential role in hobbling huge numbers of French troops. An average of about a hundred Frenchmen were now being slain by guerrillas each day. They swarmed like hornets around the communication lines, especially in the north and eastern provinces; small forts had to be surrendered because convoys were cut off; dispatches were seized; reinforcements were harried. British supplies were landed from fast frigates at lonely coves and were immediately carted into the mountains. Without the guerrillas, and without the ever-present threat from reorganised Spanish regular forces, not even Wellington could have prevented a concentration of French forces and the annihilation of the tiny British army.

Wellington now selected Salamanca as his primary target. An advance on Marmont at this city would disrupt the main enemy communications; the dispatch of French reinforcements would be hindered by guerrillas, by the threat posed by a Spanish army under Ballasteros in Soult's area, and by the presence of 17,000 Allied troops in Sicily who might descend on eastern Spain at any moment. The Cadiz garrison would continue to occupy French troops in that area, and Hill would threaten to advance along the southern corridor with 18,000 Regulars. Wellington started his advance along the northern corridor before dawn on 13 June, his 48,000 men marching in three columns. They were in excellent spirits: at last Spain was to be invaded; the real offensive had begun.

The army had been well supplied and troops carried ample

provisions – which albeit increased the burden each had to carry: biscuits and beef for three days, water, hammer, bayonet-sharpener, hatchet, camp kettle, blanket, leather for boot repairs, and a heavy rolled greatcoat perched on top of the large haversack, plus musket, bayonet, knife and eighty rounds of ball cartridge. Cavalrymen each took three days' corn and hay, spare horse-shoes and nails, and each squadron had a mobile forge. All the men were anxious to clash with the enemy again: still flushed with victory, they wanted 'to tap some more French claret'. But the enemy fell back and no serious opposition occurred before Salamanca, entered by the Allies on 17 June. Wellington besieged fortifications in the western suburbs and deployed his army around the nearby hill village of San Christobal, ready for battle with the main French force. Marmont advanced towards him on the evening of the 20th and for forty-eight hours the two armies remained within artillery range; neither commander seemed prepared to open battle first and Marmont marched away east on the 22nd. Wellington returned to the destruction of remaining French positions in the Salamanca suburbs, and these fell on the 27th.

Soon afterwards, Wellington received momentous news: Bona-parte had begun his advance into Russian territory at the beginning of the last week in June. Napoleon's dreadful and ultimately fatal 1812 campaign had started. Wellington also received a stream of other reports, from closer to hand: agents and scouts described in accurate detail the movements, composition and possible intentions of Marmont's forces. And now began three weeks of exhausting, nerve-wracking manoeuvre as each army sought the superior position to the east and south of Salamanca. 'Marmont will not risk an action,' wrote Wellington to General Graham on 3 July, 'unless he should have an advantage; and I shall certainly not risk one unless I should have an advantage.' For the Allied troops, so eagerly anticipating a victorious clash with the French, the manoeuvring became particularly wearisome; they knew nothing of the overall situation; provisions were now running short and weather conditions were terrible – fierce heat during the day, freezing cold during the night. Even Wellington complained: 'I was never so fagged.' He knew a slight slip in this deadly dance could bring swift disaster – and personal disaster almost came on 17 July when he suddenly found himself surrounded by French cavalry. Rifleman Kincaid saw his desperate escape: 'Lord Wellington, with his staff, and a cloud of French and English dragoons and horse artillery intermixed, came over the hill at full cry, and all hammering at each others' heads in one confused mass.'

By 18 July the armies had drawn close together and, according to Kincaid, 'the movements which followed presented the most beautiful military spectacle imaginable.' Both forces were massed opposite each other in full battle array. Marmont began to move south to turn the Allied flank and Wellington countered by ordering a similar southwards march. The two armies therefore moved in close parallel lines, spread across the ochre plain, regiments in formation, jingling cavalry squadrons perfectly dressed, standards fluttering. Outriders and scouts galloped along the flanks and horse-artillery detachments clattered from one position to another, from which they could fire round shot at the enemy before clattering on again. Brilliant uniforms, glittering weapons, rank upon rank of marching men, and all under the deep cloudless blue canopy, across which wheeled the mewing buzzards and circling screeching kites. A glorious, colourful spectacle it may have been – but only for romantics or those buzzards in the sky above: for the marching men, the vista seemed infinitely more restricted. All they could see were the packs of the men in front, and the churned dust ahead of their bleeding feet; prickly heavy greatcoats pressed into their necks and forced heads downwards, and thick uniform cuffs and collars chafed the skin – and the march continued for over twenty miles on the 19th and until 6 pm on the 20th, throughout the pitiless heat of the full Spanish summer. By the evening of the 20th the two armies were merely back where they had started three weeks before: the Allies around San Christobal and the French at Huerta. Marmont made another bid for the initiative on 21 July, swinging forces south across the Tormes and thus threatening both the Allied right flank and the communication links to Portugal. Wellington had to react with a similar southwards march and by nightfall both armies were across the Tormes south-east of Sala-manca. Wellington knew he would be unable to hold the city for more than a few more days: his supply lines were threatened, and already preparations had been ordered for possible retirement into Portugal, regardless of the consequent loss of prestige and damage to morale. But at dawn on the 22nd both armies still marched south-west along parallel paths towards the Arapiles hills. These rises provided the dominating positions in the area, and by 8 am manoeuvring had started for possession. Battle clearly approached.

The French seized the Greater Arapile to the east, while the Allies occupied the Lesser; meanwhile Wellington ordered his 3rd division to move out from Salamanca and take up positions at Aldea Tejada far on the Allied right. Marmont still seemed determined to stop Wellington's retreat, and to do this he had to outflank the

Troops led by General Sir Thomas Picton take the Moorish castle at Badajoz, April, 1812, and so lead the way to the allied conquest of the besieged city. Picton himself fell wounded during this terrible struggle, but recovered in time for the Battle of Vitoria in June, 1813.

The Battle of Salamanca, 27 July 1812—one of Wellington's greatest victories, fought on the hills south of the city. Wellington's tactics were superb, achieving dramatic advantages of surprise over the French under Marmont; the battle saw the beginning of the end of French domination in Spain. *Watercolour by R. Simpkin*

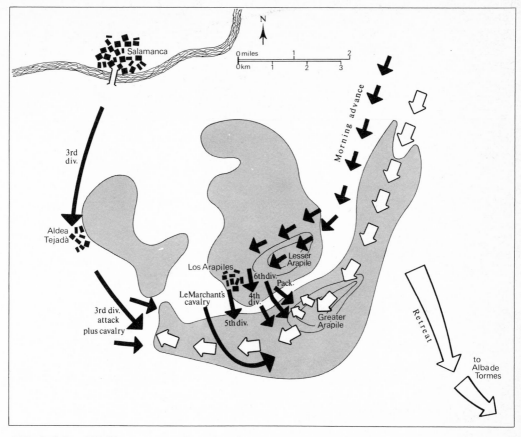

Inside map labels:
N

Salamanca

0 miles  1  2
0 km  1  2  3

Morning advance

3rd
div.

Aldea
Tejadà

Lesser
Arapile

Los Arapiles   6th div.   Pack.

Le Marchant's
cavalry         4th
                div.

3rd div.
attack
plus cavalry

5th div.

Greater
Arapile

Retreat

to
Alba de
Tormes

Allied right; Wellington, on the other hand, was willing to retire if
necessary, but was still determined to pounce upon any French
mistake – and this mistake might occur through Marmont's
speedy outflanking attempt: French forces might be over-extended
and a gap might appear in the enemy line. Wellington's hawk eyes
scanned the enemy columns as he sought his opportunity.

Alba, Spanish liaison officer on the British staff, gave a dramatic
description of Wellington's typical reaction to the crucial moment
of the day. The British commander was having late lunch at a dirty
farmyard among the brown cottages of Los Arapiles, chewing a
chicken leg while still sitting on his horse, and constantly sweeping
his shoulder he put spurs to his horse and cantered up the nearby
terrain to the east. His munches suddenly ceased. 'My God – that'll
do,' he muttered, and flinging the half-gnawed chicken bone over
his shoulder he put spurs to his horse and cantered up the nearby
slope. His telescope found the French again: the enemy army
spread over four miles – yet the left had started to move on, before
the right had been pulled up. A gap was growing between the left

Map 5   The Battle of
Salamanca, July 1812.

159

and centre columns. Wellington snapped his telescope shut, turned in his saddle to the Spanish officer and exclaimed: '*Marmont est perdu!*' No time could be lost – the French commander might soon realise his mistake; nor could any slight error or misunderstanding be allowed, and Wellington himself galloped off to give orders to the 3rd division at Aldea Tejada, commanded by Wellington's brother-in-law, Ned Pakenham. 'At them! And drive them to the devil!' he declared, then thundered back east to give similar commands to other divisions. And just before 4 pm the three columns of Pakenham's infantry, supported by Portuguese cavalry, burst from the woodlands to the west of the leading French brigade. Enemy battalions had no time to find defensive formations before cavalry charged into their ranks and 1,800 muskets scythed fire along the lines. The first French division fled back into the rest of the army. And, with the sound of rattling muskets and barking artillery from the west, Wellington's main attack was suddenly launched into the French flank. Leith's 5th division turned from the original path and with perfect precision moved into two lines each two deep, totalling 8,300 men including Portuguese units, and thrust against the second French division. Two thousand cavalry hacked in on the right and smashed five battalions of the second division, then reined to a halt, reorganised themselves, and crashed onto Marmont's third division approaching in disorder. In just thirty minutes three French divisions had been destroyed.

Action further east against remaining French units developed far more painfully. Cole's 4th division, reduced to two brigades through having to hold the Lesser Arapile, was ordered to sever the hinge in the enemy army, but to do this had to make a long advance from Los Arapiles; the men would be exposed to heavy enemy artillery fire and the 3,000 line infantrymen would have to attack two full French divisions. To help Cole, Wellington ordered Pack's brigade, 2,500 men, to storm the Greater Arapile on the left flank. Both attempts failed: Pack's Portuguese suffered severe casualties on the steep slopes and had to retreat; Cole's lines were weakened during the advance, and although his men forced back the first French positions they were repulsed by the second and fled. Wellington seemed to be everywhere, shouting encouragement, rallying those who seemed to flag. Bullets hissed about his head, and one ripped his cloak and holster. His opposite commander, Marmont, also rode in the thick of battle – and a cannonball tore into his side, flinging him yards across the ground and shattering his arms and two ribs; General Bonnet took over, and

died within minutes. General Clausel became the third com-

Sir Edward Pakenham, Wellington's brother-in-law, painted with the Battle of Salamanca as a fitting background. *From the painting by T. Heaphie.*

mander. And this newcomer conceived a brilliant movement which threatened to turn the fast-ebbing French fortune. Almost half his army had disintegrated, but the failure of the British attacks under Cole and Pack gave opportunity for a daring counter-stroke; all reinforcements were rushed into position and 12,000 Frenchmen massed to attack. Wellington had already foreseen the danger. Clinton's 6th division had already been ordered forward, and Wellington himself deployed the lines diagonally south-west from the Lesser Arapile. The French met the British in another gigantic, convulsive clash; and again the French broke first. The enemy fled the field in the dwindling daylight; Allied troops dropped exhausted in the debris, or they piled corpses to give themselves cover from the chill night wind. Wellington knew his troops were too weary for large-scale pursuit – he himself was almost dropping from tiredness – and besides he believed the Spaniards holding the Alba bridge over the Tormes would cut off the French. Not until midnight did he discover that the Spanish forces under de España had left this gateway unguarded. Nevertheless, the French probably lost over 14,000 men on the battlefield, thirty per cent of the army; Allied casualties totalled 5,214. Wellington and his army had achieved their most glorious, and bloody, victory so far. 'Everything went on as it ought,' wrote the satisfied British commander to Bathurst, 'and there never was an army so beaten in so short a time.' Wellington's reputation had now been assured. General Foy, whose division had been the only one to march from the battle with any appearance of cohesion, paid a gallant tribute to the enemy six days later. 'The battle of Salamanca

Salamanca: British troops, directed by Wellington himself, repulse Clausel's desperate counter-attack.

is the most masterly in its management . . . It raises Lord Wellington's reputation almost to the level of Marlborough.'

Pursuit was taken up on the 23rd but abandoned on the 25th, although still giving time for a brilliant charge by 450 dragoons of the King's German Legion against three French infantry battalions which left 1,400 enemy casualties. By the end of July Clausel's decimated divisions staggered along the main road towards Burgos and Vitoria; Wellington entered Valladolid on the 30th, and began his march on Madrid on 6 August. Six days later British soldiers entered the Spanish capital to find streets hung with gold and silver draperies, church bells pealing, flowers strewn before their dusty feet and bewitching Spanish maidens anxious to throw dark arms around their necks and to thrust wine into their outstretched hands. 'King' Joseph Bonaparte had already retired with his 17,000 troops, freeing the capital of French for the first time since December 1808. Hectic celebrations continued for thirty-six hours – parties, dances, love-making and drinking-bouts. Far away, Napoleon also enjoyed success, although distant clouds of disaster were already beginning to form: on 17 August, five days after Wellington entered Madrid, Bonaparte entered the burning and battered remains of Smolensk.

For fourteen days Wellington assessed the options now open to him. The French Army of the North, now under Caffarelli, was engaged against Spanish guerrillas; Hill kept French troops in the south preoccupied; in the east a Spanish army had been heavily defeated at Castalla on 21 June, but Suchet still feared Allied landings from Sicily. Clausel had turned in his tracks for a while and had chased the Spaniards from Valladolid before continuing his retreat towards Burgos. Wellington therefore had a variety of choices. While he made up his mind he attempted to solve another problem – personal finance. Madrid proved extremely expensive, and Wellington's pay amounted to only £10 a day – about £8 after deductions including income tax. 'It will be necessary,' wrote the Allied Commander-in-Chief to Bathurst on 24 August, 'that Government should now either give me an additional pay . . . or that they should allow me to charge some of the expenses . . . or I shall be ruined.'

By the end of August Wellington had decided to pursue Clausel; he left Madrid on the 31st. Six days later his army crossed the Douro and the French forces, superior in number but still de-moralised, retreated to Burgos. Wellington realised he might have to double back to Madrid at any time to help Hill against a southern threat. Yet Wellington also judged that if all went successfully he might push the main French army back almost to the Pyrenees before winter ended the campaigning season.

Matters go on well [he reported to George Murray on 7 September], and I hope before Christmas, if affairs turn out as they ought, and Boney requires all the reinforcements in the north (in Russia), to have all the gentlemen on the other side of the Ebro.

And it soon seemed Napoleon would indeed need all the help he could find: on this same day the French and Russian armies clashed at Borodino in the grim battle for Moscow; Napoleon won and entered the Russian capital seven days later, but the French in one day had lost a terrible total of 28,000 men.

Wellington reached Burgos on 18 September. Now a dangerous dilemma faced the British commander: reports showed Soult to be abandoning Andalusia in the south to join D'Erlon for a

An ice-pail featuring the Battle of Salamanca, with the towers of the city in the background. *From the Prussian Service at the Wellington Museum.*

move towards Valencia. A concentration against Madrid seemed
likely. And the old castle at Burgos had been recently strengthened
by the French into a formidable fortress. An Allied advance past
Burgos, leaving this stronghold intact in the rear, would be
extremely unwise, especially if French armies managed to concentrate. Yet to delay at Burgos in order to take the fortress would
give Clausel a chance to slip away, and the guns with the Allied
army were insufficiently strong to batter a significant breach. Once
again Wellington was being bedevilled by the sheer number of
French armies, against which not even his manoeuvring skill
could compete. He came to a rapid decision: Burgos must be taken,
despite the lack of equipment – besides, this might lure Clausel
back to a battle. Work began immediately. British troops seized
an important outpost on 19 September, yet within twenty-four
hours Wellington was writing to General Maitland: 'I doubt
however that I have the means to take the castle which is very
strong.' Wellington felt he had to persist, but increasing pessimism
penetrated his army. Rain flooded entrenchments and added to the
164 general gloom; artillery ammunition ran short; sickness multi-

plied; rats flourished; assaults launched on the 4th, 5th and 8th of October were met by ever more determined French counter-attacks. Bickering broke out among officers and brawling among the men. Another attack failed on the 18th after which Wellington declared he wanted to quit 'this damned place'. His confidence might have been slightly restored if he had known that within a day another great commander was being obliged to retreat in the face of a stubborn enemy: on 19 October Napoleon started to leave Moscow.

Wellington had already been informed of the junction of French armies under Soult, Joseph and Suchet west of Valencia; on the 19th he received a warning from Hill, now at Madrid with 36,000 men, that this force was approaching the Spanish capital. Wellington's 24,000 men were urgently required, and the regiments slipped from Burgos after dark on 21 October – Trafalgar Day. By dawn on the 22nd they had retreated ten miles to the west. Wellington's situation remained extremely dangerous. Pressing the Allied rear were 42,000 French troops under the command of Souham, who had replaced Clausel, plus 11,000 brought south by Caffarelli. The Allies were now outnumbered by about 20,000 men; many miles stretched to safety. And the army's confidence in their commander had suffered a severe jolt by the

An unknown number of French prisoners being herded into Salamanca after the battle: overall French losses totalled 14,000.

failure at Burgos; memories of the glory of Salamanca and the
entry into Madrid had been washed away by the autumn rain in
the Burgos trenches.

> Our want of success at Burgos [wrote an Ensign in the Guards] has turned
> the tide of affairs here, and Spain, I think, is lost. If ever a man ruined
> himself, the Marquis has done it. For the last two months he has acted like
> a madman . . . Such is the opinion here.

The retreat was miserable from start to finish; first the Allies withdrew behind the river Carrion, and held all three bridges across
the swollen water, then had to retreat again when Spanish troops
were forced from one of these crossings. Cabezon on the Pisuerga
river was reached on the 26th, but French troops swam across and
secured a bridgehead on the 28th. On the same day Hill retired
behind a tributary of the Tagus north of Aranjuez, his army now
in contact with the combined forces of Joseph, Jourdan and Soult –
totalling over 60,000 men. But Hill and Wellington were now only
thirty-six hours apart and soon managed to join at Salamanca. 'I
have got clear in a handsome manner, of the worst scrape I ever
was in,' wrote Wellington on the last day of this anxious month. Yet
at times his army had threatened to disintegrate into a marauding

mass: houses had been plundered *en route*, civilians molested, wine vats smashed. Sergeant Wheeler wrote:

The conduct of some men would have disgraced savages . . . It was no infrequent thing to see a long string of mules carrying drunken soldiers to prevent them falling into the hands of the enemy.

And worse had still to come.

By 8 November Wellington and Hill had concentrated their forces on a twenty-mile front from San Christobal south-east to Alba, giving a total strength of 52,000 British and Portuguese plus 18,000 Spaniards. But Soult had moved north and west to join with Souham, and Wellington estimated the enemy force to total 80,000 troops – and in fact this figure should have been at least 95,000. The enemy were unlikely to have massed such strength without intending to engage in battle; Wellington therefore waited for an assault at any moment. For seven tense days the Allies stood still while French cavalry probed their positions. Men became increasingly impatient, longing for the battle to be over and done with; provisions again ran low. Still Soult showed no signs of striking, although French formations were gathered together as if ready to move. Each day brought expectations of attack; each night men tried to snatch troubled sleep. Then, early on 15 November, the French mass began to shift slowly west to threaten Allied communications back to Ciudad Rodrigo and Portugal. Wellington countered by moving further south-east. The sinister French swing to the west continued. Wellington knew he would have to force battle against vastly superior strength, or retire, or risk his army being outflanked.

General Foy had made one comment concerning Wellington at Salamanca which had relevance now: '*Il joue serre.*' Once again he played safe: at 2 pm on the 15th he gave the order for retreat to the west, a decision which in view of the inevitable outcry from his watchful critics at home, and the grumbling of his troops, was as courageous as a command to attack. Whilst regiments withdrew from their positions, an unprecedented downpour pounded upon the demoralised troops, washing away tracks and bogging gun carriages. To ride became almost impossible; men waded nearly knee deep through the glutinous mud and cursed their commander. Wellington himself looked yellow with exhaustion. 'He wore an oilskin and looked extremely ill,' wrote an officer describing the situation on the 15th, 'which was not to be wondered at considering the anxiety of mind and fatigue of body which he was enduring.' At least rain helped keep the French at bay. Wellington reached the hamlet of Canero.

The night was dark, cold and wet [wrote one officer], and I had a severe attack of rheumatism, which added much to my distress. We had but little to eat, and nothing to drink, and it was impossible to light a fire, owing to the violence of the rain.

Misery continued on the 16th despite the continued absence of French infantry. Enemy cavalry picked up 600 Allied stragglers, and exhaustion began to paralyse even the toughest troops.

A savage sort of desperation had taken possession of our minds [reported one experienced sergeant], and those who lived on the most friendly terms in happier times now quarrelled . . . It was piteous to see some of the men, who had dragged their limbs after them with determined spirit, fall down at last among the mud . . . Numbers who had resisted the effect of hunger and fatigue with a tardy spirit were now obliged to give way, and sank to the ground praying for death to deliver them from their misery. Some prayed not in vain . . .

To keep discipline, Wellington lashed out at his troops: two men were hanged for shooting pigs, and a General Order dated 16 November declared:

The number of soldiers straggling from their regiments, for no reason excepting to plunder, is a disgrace to the army, and afford a strong proof of the degree to which discipline of the regiments is relaxed.

And yet the men had no food, owing to stores having been sent along the wrong route; and the deluge continued. Most of the men had lost their shoes and even their stockings. Three desperate divisional commanders, Dalhousie, Oswald, and William Stewart, disobeyed marching orders on the 17th and attempted to find a better route for their men – only to find themselves jammed up against an approaching Spanish army. Wellington had to lead them back to the correct road; surprisingly he contented himself with remarking: 'You see, gentlemen, I know my own business best.'

And the following evening, 18 November, the army finally arrived back in the vicinity of Ciudad Rodrigo, bruised and battered but safe again. 'My boots had not been off since the 13th,' moaned Kincaid, 'and I found it necessary to cut them to pieces, to get my swollen feet out of them.' Wellington seemed utterly depressed. He attempted to console himself by setting out the situation as he saw it in a letter to Edward Cooke, Under-Secretary for War, written on 25 November.

You will certainly be disappointed in your expectations of the result of the campaign here; and I am afraid others will be so likewise . . . Probably I ought not to have remained so long at Burgos, and ought to have withdrawn Hill at an earlier period from Madrid, and to have taken earlier measures to retire to the Agueda. [But he concluded] I played a game which might succeed (the only one which could succeed) and pushed it to the last . . . I believe I have done right.

Three days later Wellington again criticised his army, this time in a letter not intended for circulation beyond commanding officers. Discipline had been deplorable, stormed the Commander-in-Chief, worse than in any other army in which he had ever served or of which he had ever read:

Yet this army has met with no disaster; it has suffered no privations, which but trifling attention on the part of the Officers could not have prevented . . . nor has it suffered any hardships, excepting those resulting from the necessity of being exposed to the inclemencies of the weather.

The contents of the letter soon became known to the troops; morale slumped even lower and discontent increased. The army, and the atmosphere within it, seemed in complete contrast to that of only four months before: men had been plunged from the heady heights of victory. And yet Wellington, despite his generalisation, was partially correct in his criticism: the army had not suffered disaster nor even defeat. Although the advance had failed and men were back at their starting point, the situation had been changed. Wellington and his troops had freed southern Spain; the French concentration against the Allied army helped guerrillas elsewhere. Moreover, Allied depression soon proved only skin-deep and had disappeared within a few days: warmth, food, clean clothes, new boots and reasonable comfort in winter quarters revived optimism and brought back better memories; as the resilient troops sat with their pipes around their fires they gossiped not about the recent miseries but the victories at Ciudad Rodrigo, Badajoz, Salamanca . . .

The position was far different for the French. They might have regained ground, but were still on the run. French memories could only be sour, all of them concerning defeats which had been suffered despite superior manpower. And dreadful reports began to filter over the Pyrenees: Napoleon's army in Russia had been suffering terrible losses throughout November; Ney's corps of 9,000 men had been sacrificed at Krasnoi on the 16th and 17th, with only 800 survivors; thousands more French had perished at the icy Beresina between the 26th and 28th; the Emperor quit the remains of the army on 8 December, and when survivors stumbled back over the Russian border, only about 10,000 effective fighting men could be counted – 450,000 had advanced to fight less than six months before.

This monstrous defeat would constitute a crushing burden even for Napoleon's bull neck, and Wellington and his men rested content in their winter quarters around Ciudad Rodrigo. Omens were good.

# Chapter 8

# To the
# Streets of Toulouse

Wellington had to find an answer to his great strategical problem: his army could beat the enemy in battle, providing he took no undue risks and chose positions which would best serve his divisions' superb strength under fire and disciplined counter-volleys; he knew the French to be demoralised. And yet the enemy had the overriding advantage of greater numbers: his army had been obliged to withdraw by the multiple forces which began to concentrate immediately the Allies advanced. The British Commander-in-Chief studied maps, plans and reports during the winter months; and he found his answer. Meanwhile his men continued to rest and to train – soon they would need to call upon the maximum benefits derived from both. And if Wellington felt any quickening emotion he took care to control it; he remained as starchy as before, even when spring, 1813, brought so many promises in the honeysuckle-scented air. A member of his staff reported remarks made by Wellington on Sunday, 4 April, that

his men were now all so round-shouldered and slouching in their gait, that he was sure, if his regiment here was in its present state to pass in review at Wimbledon Common, the whole would be sent to drill immediately, and declared quite unfit for service.

But when Wellington reviewed his troops early in May they seemed much improved – at least in the eyes of Rifleman Kincaid.

It did one's very heart good to look at our battalion that day . . . each daring, bronzed countenance, which looked you boldly in the face, in the fullness of vigour and confidence, as if it cared neither for man nor devil.

The time had come to move. Regiments had been drilled and exercised until each battalion could move from column into line formation or from line into square in thirty seconds, regardless of terrain; discipline had been tightened; medical services improved; tents issued; greater marching mobility achieved by scrapping heavy greatcoats and substituting lighter pots for the heavy iron kettles. Men, like muskets, were primed to fight. But the enemy remained strong. Suchet, north of Valencia, had up to 70,000 men; Clausel in the north had about 30,000; and three armies were in central Spain under Gazan, D'Erlon and Reille, totalling 100,000 infantry and cavalry. Few men had been taken from Spain despite the Russian catastrophe – and, in central Europe, Napoleon seemed to have temporarily turned the tide again, fighting with his old brilliance at Lutzen on 2 May and again at Bautzen on the 20th and 21st.

*Opposite* Joseph's headlong retreat after his coach had been surrounded – leaving his treasure and personal belongings in the hands of the British.

Also on the 21st the Allied army in Spain broke up from winter quarters. Wellington's plan soon became plain. He intended to use one advantage which could be obtained through having a small, outnumbered army: speed. He would by-pass central Spain and strike hard and fast towards the most sensitive part of the enemy territory – the north, towards the Pyrenees and France. All being well, the enemy would be thrown off balance and the Allied army would streak on, before the French could concentrate. Hence all his preparations for greater mobility. Hill was ordered to march by the Tagus valley, as if making for Madrid, and for further camouflage Wellington divided his own force into two unequal parts: he led the smaller contingent of 30,000 men against Salamanca to deceive the enemy into thinking this was his principal thrust – a disproportionately large cavalry force would give a thicker screen, while General Graham took the main force of 60,000 men through the mountain wilderness of Tras os Montes in the north, to outflank the waiting French on the Douro. All went according to the rigid plan. Salamanca fell on the 26th; Hill, who had now swerved north to join Wellington, was left in command, and Wellington himself dashed off to join Graham on the 29th. This northern route had previously been considered impassable by the French, and they were almost proved correct. Unexpected rains had swollen the Esla, flowing south into the Douro, to make a crossing apparently out of the question. But Wellington urged troops forward: the first men surged through the slushy foam clinging to stirrups and tails of cavalry mounts; a swaying pontoon bridge was erected, and the army pressed on. By the evening of 3 June, Wellington had his entire force of 100,000 men united at Toro, north of the Douro, while the French, realising too late that the entire Allied army was not at Salamanca, were withdrawing north and desperately trying to concentrate forces. Wellington refused to allow them sufficient time. At 7 am on the 13th the French blew up the Burgos magazine and abandoned the fortress; within sixty minutes of hearing the explosions, Wellington's columns were ordered to swing north-east and north, to outflank the French and to avoid defensive traps on the main road, while Spanish lancers under Sanchez would continue to prod the French along the direct route. Once again the French found themselves outwitted: they had believed these northern alternative routes to be impossible for an army with artillery; Wellington, sifting evidence from scouts during the winter, knew otherwise.

Here was Wellington at his brilliant best. Joseph's armies had hoped to find defensive positions on the river Ebro, but Wellington's

main forces struck north over the mountains to outflank the enemy again, his men sliding on the slippery shale, dragging mules and gun-carriages, hurrying through countryside devoid of vegetation or even soil, and then, abruptly, the troops were looking down on the broad, lush, romantic valley of the Ebro; down the slopes they went, still moving northwards until they reached Villarcayo and Medina de Pomar on the 15th and 16th, when Wellington wheeled his regiments to the east. The Commander-in-Chief seemed everywhere, first with one column, then another, handling the Light Division himself against the French at San Millan on the 18th, then rushing to Graham's flanking troops. Ever back went the French, pressed from the rear and menaced from their flank. One biblical corporal in the Horse Guards commented: 'The French, with might, haste and vigour, did slip from one mountain to another before we had scarcely time to count the valleys.' Captured prisoners confirmed the enemy confusion. And the guerrillas acted as superb partners in this whirling, hectic campaign: three French squadrons were now needed to protect normal couriers, even on a good road, and when Joseph had sent desperate orders from Burgos on the 9th, instructing Clausel to join him, 1,500 men had escorted the messenger – although the order arrived, Clausel's

Troops under Murray fight against Suchet at Valencia, after having sailed 300 miles up the coast. With Suchet preoccupied, Wellington could push after Joseph.

173

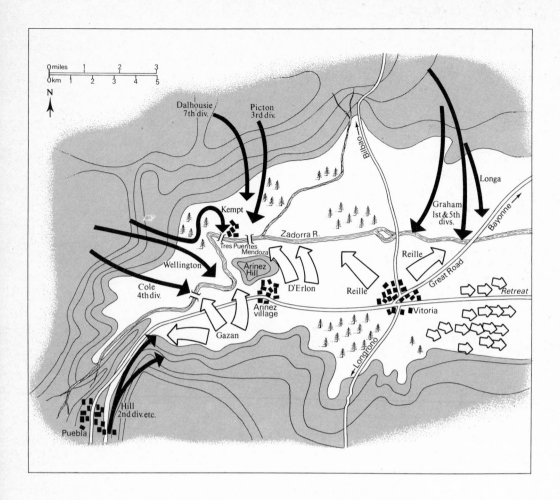

Map 6  The Battle of
Vitoria, June 1813.

answering dispatch failed to make it. Wellington knew more about
the whereabouts of the French armies than the French did themselves: Clausel was moving north from Pamplona, but would be
unlikely to be able to reach Joseph until at least the 22nd; the Allied
army totalled just over 70,000 and had a slight numerical
advantage over Joseph's force. The latter had been pushed north,
off-balance and in disorder; now Joseph must be brought to battle
before Clausel could arrive. By 19 June both Wellington and the
French were in the vicinity of the Zadorra valley. French troops
were snatching rest in the western area, and Joseph would be
reluctant to move on, further from Clausel, until the confusion of
convoys could be sorted out at Vitoria in the centre of the
rectangular valley. Wellington halted his troops on the 20th in
bivouac areas on the eastern hills and waited for Graham's column
to come up on the left. The British commander had completed

174

Wellington at Salamanca; during the battle the British commander seemed to be everywhere at once, and always where most needed. With him on the dark horse in this painting is the under-rated General William Carr Beresford; immediately after Salamanca Beresford fell wounded by a musket shot from an allied sentry.

The 'Battles of the
Pyrenees', July and
August, 1813—the two
main clashes against
Soult's twin offensives.
Fought in terrible
terrain, these actions
cost the French over
13,000 casualties, but as
Wellington remarked:
'It was a close run
thing.' Now the British
leader could prepare for
his next move—a strike
into France.

British forces cross into
France over the Bidassoa
river, October, 1813.
Wellington had
discovered that the
river could be forded
nearer to the sea than
the French had realised.

Joseph Bonaparte, sent scurrying northwards by Wellington's lightning advance, and soon to be humiliated at Vitoria. *From the painting by Baron Gerard.*

preparations by the time 21 June dawned, cold and drizzling.

Joseph seemed to be expecting an attack from the west over the Zadorra river. Wellington had more subtle plans. He himself would lead two columns down from the hills in the west, but not until two more British assaults had punched into the French line from left and right – Hill's column would attack on the left by thrusting south-west along the main road through the gaunt Puebla defile, while Graham's force would swing in from the north-east, under cover of the hills, into the opposite corner of the valley. He would roll back the French right and sever the French retreat along the Great Road to Bayonne. Troops under Dalhousie and Picton would also move behind the mountains before swinging south and stabbing slightly to the right of the French centre. The plan sounded easy in theory when arrows were scribbled across tattered maps. Practice would be far more difficult: Graham would 177

Vitoria: Wellington deploys his units to seize upon the unexpected weakness in the French lines.

be twelve miles from Hill and eight miles from his nearest support; the windy mountains around Vitoria were rugged, trackless and swept by mist; the valley itself was uneven, blotted with pine-woods and slashed by the winding Zadorra.

Wellington's troops waited shivering in the dreary early daylight on the 21st while Hill and Graham began their attacks. 'Daddy' Hill opened at 8.30, sending brave Spaniards and kilted High-landers swarming along the precipices on his right and thundering along the main road against Gazan's defences. Within thirty minutes Graham had started to probe at the distant end of the valley. Throughout the morning, as the sun pierced the mist and the shadows shortened, Allied troops forced their way steadily forward at each end of the French army. The German com-missary officer, Schaumann, waxed eloquent:

The bright morning sunshine, the gloomy wooded hills, the flash of the muskets, the rolling thunder of the fire, and the wonderful shapes formed by smoke in and out of the groups of trees covering the hills, lent a picturesque grandeur to the scene.

Most of the troops under Wellington's direct command still awaited the order to advance; they sat on their knapsacks on the hillsides, protected by ridges, and from the distance they appeared

178

as huge red blotches against the greens and browns of the scrub. Just before noon Wellington made an important alteration to his plans: a Spanish peasant revealed that the bridge across the Zadorra at Tres Puentes remained undefended, and, because the river at this point swung behind the Arinez knoll, a crossing would be unobserved by the French until almost the last minute. Wellington immediately ordered Kempt's brigade of the Light Division to advance and follow the Zadorra round to this bridge.

Meanwhile the fourth Allied thrust, by troops under Dalhousie and Picton from the north, had been delayed. Dalhousie had found difficulty in marching through the broken country, although Picton's 3rd division was in position just before noon after a more southerly approach. Picton himself, smartly dressed in blue coat and fashionable round hat, squirmed with impatience in his creaking saddle. Unable to understand the delay he snapped: 'Damn it! Lord Wellington must have forgotten us.' His men grumbled at the inactivity; Picton irritably poked at his horse's mane with his stick. Up galloped an *aide-de-camp*: Picton would remain in reserve while Dalhousie's 7th division attacked, supported by the 4th and 6th. Picton flung back his head in anger and almost stood in his stirrups. 'You may tell Lord Wellington from me, Sir,' he spluttered at the startled messenger, 'that the 3rd division under my command shall in less than ten minutes attack the bridge and carry it, and the 4th and 6th divisions may support, if they so choose.' He dragged round his horse, galloped to the front of his men and shouted: 'Come on ye rascals! Come on ye fighting villains!' And the whole battle exploded into terrible crescendo.

Picton's raging storm of cheering troops swept down into the valley, joined by Dalhousie's first arrivals, and fell upon Mendoza bridge across the Zadorra; Kempt's brigade from the Light Division hit the Tres Puentes bridge just to the right. The rest of the Light Division and the 4th struck direct at Gazan's main positions further south along the river. Hill continued his clash with Gazan's left flank. Graham had already slashed the exit road from the valley in the north-east and pushed on towards Vitoria. Picton's wave of men washed over the bridge and around the knoll and village of Arinez. Gazan managed to throw up a defensive line in this area; by 3 pm this had been thrust aside by Wellington in personal command of the 3rd division, by Kempt's brigade and by part of Dalhousie's 7th. Crashing artillery salvoes shuddered the soil beneath the struggling troops and billowed smoke over the battlefield, but each time the gunfire abated the French could be seen falling back towards Vitoria.

In all directions there was nothing but fire [wrote Schaumann], smoke, moving columns, troops forming squares or occupying conquered heights, dead and wounded men and horses, and shelled houses and trees; while weapons of all kinds, forage caps, strips of uniform, cartridge boxes, paper cases, buttons and shoes covered the ground.

Files of men ran through the fields, bayonets glinting above the uncut crop; moments later they had come under fire, and blood splattered over the yellow corn, earth vomited skywards and mangled men crawled for non-existent cover. Horses ran whinnying among the retreating troops, riderless or dragging their battered owners by the stirrup-irons; it was, according to the hardened Kincaid, 'a scene of extraordinary and exhilarating interest.'

Wellington threw in Cole's 4th division, still comparatively fresh, and this sliced between Gazan's and D'Erlon's disintegrating divisions. Back went the French, leaving blackened cannon bogged up to their hubs in marshy streams – each gun with a once-proud name carved upon the barrel: *Egalité, Liberté, Fortune* . . . Men sought temporary safety by flinging themselves into ditches and behind walls.

At one period [remembered Kincaid], we held one side of a wall . . . while the French were on the other side, so that any person who chose to put his head over from either side was sure of getting a sword or a bayonet up his nostrils. The situation was, of course, too good to be of long endurance. The same features which had made Wellington's strategy in the 1813 campaign so successful were now repeated tactically at Vitoria: the French were kept off-balance and on the run by swift-moving, outflanking, supremely confident Allied troops. Ditch to ditch, wall to wall, house to house, they retreated, and the further and faster the retreat, the more the French became stricken with panic. Packs were tossed away, then muskets and ammunition and swords; baggage carts and ornate polished carriages were tumbled to one side. The streets of Vitoria were blocked with gun-carriages, dead horses and ever-mounting rubble, and men had to scramble over these obstacles before they could race through the gardens and vineyards beyond. The main road to Bayonne remained blocked by Graham's forces; the French took to the fields to the east.

Most of them managed to escape, although only two guns could be rescued. Broken terrain favoured retreat and men of Reille's two divisions managed to maintain a rearguard defence. But the principal reason for the mass French escape lay in the diversion now offered to the victorious Allied troops: apart from losing almost all his artillery, Joseph had been obliged to leave

behind his 3,000 convoy wagons, carriages and carts – and he himself had to flee on foot after his coach had been surrounded. The resulting loot had magnetic attraction, from Joseph's glittering silver chamber pot to the vast piles of coins which clattered from the shattered chests. Humble British troops filled their pockets and packs and staggered away far richer men, among them Sergeant Costello of the 95th who netted over £1,000, a private of the 23rd who carried off 1,000 silver dollars, and two soldiers of the 68th who gathered 180 doubloons and nearly 1,000 dollars respectively. Acres around Vitoria were littered with jewels, sackfuls of candlesticks, silver teapots, silver ingots, precious plate, knives, forks and spoons, and a multitude of twinkling trinkets. Amongst the muddy treasure lay a chamberlain's coat of blue velvet and gold lace, King Joseph's sporting guns inlaid with gold, and his silk underclothing embroidered with a red J surmounted by a tiny crown. Other

Finding the main road to Bayonne blocked, the panic-stricken French forces retreat across the fields to the east of Vitoria.

181

"More TROPHIES for White-hall !?!"

Vitoria – the fruits of victory, and also the reason for the delay in mounting the Allied pursuit of the French.

spoils of war were soon discovered; Schaumann reported:

The unmarried ladies belonging to the French army, most of whom were young and good-looking Spanish women, dressed in fancy hussar uniforms and mounted on pretty ponies . . . were first robbed of their mounts, their carriages and their jewels, and then most ungallantly allowed to go. But, as all they wanted was protection and a new lover, both of which they soon obtained, they were to be had for the asking.

Young officers caroused that night at a feast prematurely organised by the French in Vitoria to celebrate their victory over the Allies: crisp roast mutton, a variety of fowl and a perfect succession of wines – Médoc, Burgundy, Champagne. Participants ate until dull weariness overcame them, then they slumped in their seats, flung themselves on the floor, or lay amidst the dinner debris on the table, still wearing boots, spurs, and bloodstained equipment. By dawn on 22 June most of the army seemed in a thick stupor of exhaustion or drunkenness, and even when roused the lethargy continued. Pursuit became further delayed. Men had to be rounded up – more men were lost in temporary desertion in search of plunder than had fallen in the battle. Wellington paced his field headquarters in rage and dictated a vicious dispatch.

182

We started with the army in the highest order, and up to the day of the battle nothing could get on better; but that event has, as usual, totally annihilated all order and discipline . . . We may gain the greatest victories; but we shall do no good until we shall so far alter our system, as to force all ranks to perform their duty.

The French had lost only 756 men killed in battle, although a further 7,200 were wounded or missing – compared with an Allied overall total of 5,148 – yet this low fatality figure underlined the supremacy of the Allied army: victory had been achieved without mass bloodshed. As Wellington put it: 'The two armies were nearly equal in numbers, but they cannot stand us now at all.' On the other hand, the vast numbers of enemy survivors increased the need for speedy pursuit, before they could reorganise and while morale remained shattered. Clausel reached the Vitoria area late on the 22nd, learnt of the disastrous battle, and retired the way he had come, before turning north-east towards Pamplona. Wellington's main army was also moving on Pamplona on the 23rd, but by now Joseph's forces had retreated on towards the French border, only a day's march away, leaving a garrison in the city. Clausel avoided a trap on the north bank of the Ebro and followed Joseph across the frontier into France. Enemy troops flooded through the Pyrenean passes, leaving Suchet's army isolated in the far south-east. By the end of the month only three enemy pockets remained in northern Spain: the town of Vera and the fortresses at San Sebastian and Pamplona. Wellington had virtually cleared the French from Spain in a brilliant two-month campaign.

Outside events now clamoured for consideration. Napoleon, pursuing the Prussians and Russians east of the Elbe, had found the Allies growing in strength while his communications became stretched and his reserves dwindled. He needed time for re-organisation. Austria remained neutral but her Foreign Minister, Metternich, urged war against the French – and an army of 200,000 was being raised. On 1 June Napoleon had entered Breslau, and on the same day his request for an armistice was agreed to by the Allies, officially to discuss peace at Prague; five days later this northern truce had been extended until 20 July, later to 16 August. On 26 June Napoleon met Metternich in an attempt to discuss terms for a treaty which would keep Austria out of the war; Metternich countered by making preposterous demands and 183

Austria signed the Treaty of Reichenbach between Prussia and Austria on the 27th: the Allies told Napoleon to agree to Metternich's demands by 10 July – later extended to 10 August – or face an Austrian declaration of war. If the armistice were further extended, or if Napoleon came to temporary terms in the north, reinforcements could be rushed to southern France and an advance by Wellington would be caught exposed. On the other hand Wellington could establish himself by the Pyrenees and prevent another French advance into Spain, regardless of the current position in northern Europe. Wellington therefore decided to consolidate his hold south of the frontier: a thrust into France would be delayed until the situation cleared in the north. 'I hope we shall soon have San Sebastian,' wrote the British commander to Bathurst on 12 July, 'and if we get settled in the Pyrenees, it will take a good reinforcement to the French army to drive us from thence.'

Wellington apparently still seethed over the behaviour of his troops after Vitoria, and felt it necessary to express his feeling to Bathurst on 2 July. 'We have in the service the scum of the earth as common soldiers.' Wellington later received shocked criticism for these sacrilegious words; on the other hand he gave no indication that he considered all his troops in the same bad light, and he could have been referring to the recruiting material from which the soldiers came, and not the finished product; later, in 1831, he added a significant sentence to the same statement:

The French system of conscription brings together a fair sample of all classes; ours is composed of the scum of the earth – the mere scum of the earth. It is only wonderful that we should be able to make so much of them afterwards.

Nevertheless, Wellington felt the need for a General Order on 9 July, warning against riotous or revengeful behaviour when the time came to move into France itself: French citizens 'should be well treated, and private property must be respected'. On the same day he scribbled another letter to Bathurst: 'I do not know what measures to take about our vagabond soldiers. By the state of yesterday, we had 12,500 men less under arms than we had on the day before the battle.' The call to arms for further action against the French would bring the wanderers into the ranks, and on 15 July troops concentrated again to clear the enemy from Vera. Only San Sebastian and Pamplona remained in French hands. But also on the 15th Wellington received confirmation that the able and experienced Soult had replaced Joseph as commander of the French forces over the border, and reports also arrived of an imminent French offensive. The enemy would enjoy the initiatives of time and direction for the attack; numerous places existed in the Pyrenees through which an army could march and Wellington could not block each one. He aimed instead to concentrate his forces after the enemy advance had begun.

An attempt to storm San Sebastian had been planned for 24 July, but was postponed to the 25th. Wellington was informed at 11.30 am on this day that the attack had failed, and immediately hurried off to see the situation for himself. At that same time Soult had launched his offensive into Spain. While Wellington gave fresh orders at San Sebastian, French forces were advancing to relieve Pamplona in a two-pronged attack through the mountains: D'Erlon advanced with 21,000 men towards Maya, while Soult accompanied Clausel's 40,000 towards Roncesvalles.

Hill commanded the troops in the Maya region, and had assigned the defence of the nearby pass to two brigades of the 2nd division – Cameron's and Stewart's, the latter being commanded by Pringle at the time. Enemy units had been seen moving to the north early on the 25th, but inadequate watch was being maintained – Pringle's men were anyway inefficiently deployed for observation. At 10 am a line of 700 *tirailleurs*, backed by strong French columns, suddenly attacked Pringle's companies and within forty minutes had forced them from their positions. The enemy swept through the pass and into the valley beyond. British troops tried desperately to stem the flood: four hundred men of the 92nd, the Gordon Highlanders, stood forward on a tiny hummock to receive the full blow of an entire French division, and they did so for twenty terrible minutes.

They stood there like a stone wall [wrote one officer], overmatched by 20 to 1, until half their blue bonnets lay beside those brave northern warriors. When they retired, their dead bodies lay as a barrier to the advancing foe. Oh but they did fight well that day; I can see the line now of the killed and wounded stretched upon the heather.

Fighting continued throughout the day with unit after unit thrown forward against vastly superior numbers. Then, at about 6 pm, British reinforcements arrived from the west and counter-attacked – with surviving Gordon Highlanders joining the assault despite orders to stay. 'The pipe-major was not to be denied. He struck up the charging tune of "The Haughs of Cromdale", his comrades . . . not only charged but led the charge.' French troops were pushed back to the pass, allowing the British to withdraw in good order to the Baztan valley. But twenty miles away over the rugged mountains, the British had suffered defeat on the twin

ridges above Roncesvalles. Clausel's initial attack, made along the
east spur, failed to make good progress, while Reille's troops
working their way along the west were blocked along the narrow
crest. Then, between 4 and 5 pm, low cloud settled over the
positions, and the British commander, Sir Lowry Cole, became
increasingly anxious in the eerie stillness. He feared the enemy's
40,000 would creep forward in the covering mist to envelop his
slim force of 13,000. And Cole lost his nerve. Despite Wellington's
orders to hold on whatever the cost, he gave the command for
retreat.

Yet first reports to reach Wellington at San Sebastian seemed re-
assuring, and he retired for the night. Just over two hours later he
was roused by the first news of the true situation: Pamplona had
been the real objective, and the Allied holding line had broken.
Wellington jumped from his couch, called for his horse, and

galloped south. Reports received *en route* revealed further bad news, and Wellington even left his staff behind in his haste to reach the threatened area. British troops under Cole and Picton had been drawn up on a ridge to the south-east of Sorauren village, ten miles from Pamplona itself; Clausel's troops were already moving over the rise just opposite and any moment would filter into the houses of Sorauren – Wellington reached the village on his lathered horse just as the French advanced up the road on the other side. He barely had time to stop, scribble orders for reinforcements, thrust them to his sole remaining aide, and gallop away up to the British troops on the hillsides. Men recognised him as he rode past and the call ran down the line: 'Nosey has come! See – old Nosey! Nosey!' Nervous and unsettled a few minutes before, now they stood and cheered, waved their hats and flourished muskets in the air. Wellington made the most of it. He positioned himself on a prominent rock, levelled his spy-glass and calmly viewed the French: if the tumult and cheering in the British lines confused the enemy, so much the better – the able but indecisive Soult might believe British reinforcements had arrived. Through his telescope Wellington could pick out the enemy commander and his staff; French troops still moved in columns and had yet to be deployed, and Wellington concluded time might still be allowed for Pack's 6th division to reach the scene before battle began. Moreover, O'Donnell's force of Spaniards at nearby Pamplona had been re-deployed to free a full division for Picton's use, and Hill should be withdrawing along the road from Maya towards the battle area. But in the early evening these reinforcement plans received a serious setback when thunderclouds broke upon the mountains, and a deluge poured down the howling Pyrenean passes to delay marching troops.

Yet the storm also brought darkness and a thankful end to the day. Even the following morning, 28 July, Soult remained apparently undecided. Not until almost noon did the French attack, and by then Pack's division had started to enter the valley to the south of Sorauren. French battalions thrust forward to block his advance and fierce fighting spread along the whole line. Within minutes the battle became a crackling clash of grinding battalions: the British stood firm against repeated French attacks and the path to Pamplona remained blocked. 'The 28th was fair bludgeon-work,' wrote Wellington. Both sides rested from sheer exhaustion on the 29th; battle resumed on the 30th but fighting had ceased before noon with the Allies still in possession. Hill had been engaged with D'Erlon on the extreme Allied left, but managed to

*The Battle of Vitoria.*
*From an urn in the*
*Prussian Service at the*
*Wellington Museum.*

keep his forces intact despite loss of ground. French corpses lay thick among the gorse, already blackened by the scorching sun; enemy casualties from Soult's twin offensives totalled at least 13,500 out of the original 60,000 troops. The Allies had lost 7,100. These 'Battles of the Pyrenees' had been expensive, and the scare had been acute: Wellington admitted: 'At one time it was alarming, certainly, and it was a close run thing.' But now Soult's sword had been shattered, and the French were retreating towards the border with Hill in pursuit. Once again the French managed to escape, due to Soult's good management and to missed opportunities, and as usual Wellington criticised the chase. By then the British commander felt far from well, suffering from lumbago and from general weariness after fighting in this incredibly tough campaigning country.

But at least the recent battles had revealed to the French that another attempt to occupy Spain would be extremely hazardous and costly, and the enemy retired to lick their wounds. Moreover, tremendous events were happening in central and northern Europe and rumours were already filtering into the French camp, the contents of which would make the enemy hesitate to move on to the offensive again. News of these events would take another month to reach Wellington, but he too preferred to rest quiet for the moment. Operations against San Sebastian continued throughout August, and by the last week the fortress had clearly almost reached its end. Soult made a further relief attempt on the 31st but this was

The siege of San Sebastian, last main French stronghold in north Spain and sole remaining obstacle to Wellington's advance into France.

189

Graham's troops storm San Sebastian, August 1813; with the capitulation of the city on 5 September came charges of barbarism levelled against Wellington.

blocked by Spanish troops under Freire and the enemy soon withdrew again. And on the same day Allied troops stormed San Sebastian following five days' heavy bombardment: after vigorous final defence the French garrison pulled back to the castle, which eventually capitulated on 5 September. The town itself suffered severely from fire soon after the assault on the 31st; Wellington was accused in Spanish newspapers of having ordered the burning – a blatantly false charge: if the British commander had wished to raze the town by fire he would surely have done so before the attack, thus saving 3,700 Allied casualties.

At last, on 3 September, tremendous European news arrived. On 10 August the Austrians had finally plucked up sufficient courage and had entered the war against France. Two days before this, the armistice had been renounced by Russia and Prussia, and Wellington heard that hostilities were likely to be resumed at any moment. In fact fighting had already broken out again, unknown to the British commander. But he knew the time had nearly come for the Allies to strike into southern France; nearly, but not quite. Pamplona neared starvation, and Wellington could afford to stay a while longer for more definite information of active campaigning in the north, so, as he waited for the right moment to move, he prepared his troops and tried to settle countless petty problems with the Spanish authorities. The bulk of the Allied army remained concentrated behind the Bidassoa river, with Wellington's HQ in the small, dirty village of Lesaca, eight miles south-east of Irún. For the troops, life was quiet and relatively comfortable, except for the rain and the attempts of 'do-gooders' from home to improve their spiritual well-being. 'It is a melancholy fact,' declared one report, 'that in the 23rd regiment it would be difficult at times to procure even one English Bible, and this scarcity I believe exists throughout the whole army in the Peninsula.' Contact with the French became infrequent; as Kincaid commented: 'Between the French and us there was no humbug, it was either peace or war. The war, on both sides, was conducted on the grand scale, and, by a tacit sort of understanding, we never teased each other unnecessarily.'

This 'grand scale' broke out again on 7 October 1813. By now the war had been resumed in central Europe on an awesome level: the Allies had taken the field with armies totalling over 520,000 men, and Napoleon, although managing to assemble 442,000 front-line troops, would clearly be unable to send reinforcements to the south. Indeed, strength in this area might soon be reduced. And Wellington unleashed his forces.

French battalions lining the far bank of the Bidassoa would be the first obstacle, followed by the climb up to the great Pyrenean spine; then would come the Nivelle and Nive rivers before Bayonne. Wellington aimed to repeat his successful tactics: rapid movement, outflanking attacks, constant leaps forward. And at exactly 7.25 am on the 7th the advance commenced. Three batteries of British guns signalled the start: shells ripped into the early morning fog and Allied troops began to move. Humble Spanish shrimpers unlocked the door, leading British troops across the Bidassoa estuary into France; on they tramped through the muddy, shallow water, and by 11.30 am the French had been outflanked. Columns could be seen withdrawing up into the mountains and on to the majestic

191

Wellington and his staff
watch British troops
wade across the shallow
waters of the Bidassoa
estuary into France.

Great Rhune which dominated the area. Spanish attempts to take these heights failed, but Wellington maintained the momentum of the advance: Allied troops outflanked the Great Rhune on 8 October and by evening the line of the Pyrenees had been broken. Wellington calmly continued to hold his impetuous young officers in check: the advance must be controlled, and now he wanted to wait for the fall of Pamplona before making his next move. Dogs, cats and rats were known to be fetching high prices within the besieged French garrison. Meanwhile Wellington organised his men, ordered improvements to be made to roads, studied the terrain ahead from his excellent vantage-point on the Great Rhune, while his men waited in pouring winter rain. Lieutenant Edmund Wheatley, King's German Legion, wrote in his diary on the 12th: 'The rains are so very violent just now that the dead bodies from the battle last week have swelled and protruded from the earth. One fellow's hand is now out at the back of my tent and from the buttons I see he is of the 9th Regiment.' Soon the thunderstorms would become almost as much an enemy as the French.

Pamplona capitulated at the end of October. Wellington waited a few more days to allow the snow-delayed arrival of Hill's troops from the Roncesvalles area and to give his men greater practice in night marching, an essential feature for the Battle of the Nivelle. Units were ordered to prepare to move at 3 am on 10 November. Baggage and tents were collected and sent to the rear; men stood around their fires for another hour; then came the quiet order to move. Nothing could be heard but dull rattling as muskets were unhooked, and the men filed into the dark carrying their weapons horizontally to prevent bayonets gleaming in the intermittent moonlight. Wheatley spared one last glance at the remains of the camp. 'Fires stood deserted, excepting a solitary drummer boy shivering with apprehension and cold, or a soldier kneeling to the fire, lighting perhaps his last pipe . . .' Down the sides of the Great Rhune crept the British files and around the flank of the Lesser Rhune, where French positions were embedded in the rocks and ravines. Signal guns shattered the silence as the first sun-rays played above the mountain ridges, and the Light Division leapt from their nooks and crannies, ran half a mile over marshy ground, and took the first French line; five minutes later they went on again, up the narrow paths, stabbing and throwing aside opposition until they reached the crest, while further to the north more British troops drove back skirmishers. By 8 am the Lesser Rhune had been taken. Nine Allied divisions immediately advanced to the east; the Nivelle was crossed; village after village fell as the Allies surged daily forward and the French retreated to the Nive. By 16 November Bayonne had been uncovered.

Activity died down again for another three weeks: time in which to prepare for the next burst forward. Now the Allies had the mountains at their backs and victory seemed over the next horizon – or the next. Wellington had interviewed a French prisoner: where, he had asked, were the Emperor Napoleon's present headquarters? 'My Lord,' came the startling reply, 'there are no more headquarters.' In this way the British commander received information of the 'Battle of the Nations' fought at Leipzig between 16 and 19 October when Napoleon had received his first decisive defeat in a European battle. By 9 November the French leader had fled back to Paris. Wellington allowed himself a rare smile of satisfaction: 'I see my way clearly to Bordeaux and Paris.' But the very success of the Allies in Germany brought problems for Wellington with his allies in southern France. The local political situation deteriorated rapidly, with the Spaniards causing more than their usual amount of trouble: Napoleon had thrown out tempting offers – he would restore Ferdinand to the Spanish throne in return for a virtual Spanish military alliance against Britain. At the same time, Wellington's Spanish troops took it upon themselves to avenge the barbaric treatment their countrymen had suffered at the hands of the French occupation troops. Local French people were molested; Spanish malcontents plundered the village of Ascain, slaughtering civilians. Wellington knew this could be disastrous: he needed the cooperation, or at least the acquiescence, of the French population, and he sent the most unruly Spanish battalions back over the Pyrenees. Schaumann witnessed their departure: 'They made a dreadful tumult as they marched along. Their hatred of the English, and particularly Lord Wellington, who had them hanged whenever they robbed . . . manifested itself.' Hatred was reciprocated among the men. 'A Spanish officer,' wrote Wheatley in his diary on the 29th, 'begged just now for a night's lodging in my room, which I refused for I hate a Spaniard more than a Frenchman.'

Wellington's infantry force now totalled 36,000 British, 23,000 Portuguese and 4,000 better-disciplined Spanish troops under Morillo. Soult outnumbered the Allies by a few hundred. And now the Nive had to be crossed, wider than the Nivelle and swollen with the torrential November rain. As before, final preparations took place in the dark of night. Suddenly, just before dawn on 9 December, a beacon flared into life, and the Allies advanced to the river over a four-mile front. Spies had reported three fords which could still be crossed, although not without difficulty and danger. Troops under Hill forced their way through the currents to the far bank. Further north, flimsy pontoon bridges had been constructed during darkness: Beresford's 3rd and 6th divisions tramped across. Sheets of rain still swept the sodden fields, but the Allied advance moved with customary speed. Soult fell back towards Bayonne itself, while Wellington sent Hope with three divisions and three brigades to strike between the Nive and the sea. By evening the Allies had formed a semi-circle around Bayonne, but French opposition stiffened. And still the rain came down; troops were unable to keep bivouac fires alight and spent the night huddled in dripping misery. Soult counter-attacked at 9 am on the 10th, but the Allied grip held; fighting dwindled on the 11th, only to increase again on the 12th. And that night troops in Hill's force on the Allied right, to the south-east of the city, could hear rumbling wheels over the Bayonne bridges as Soult shifted units towards their three-mile front. At 8 am on the 13th packed enemy masses could be seen advancing. Never had 'Daddy' Hill's reliability and resilience been so required as they were on this day – he actually swore, for only the second time in the Peninsular War: for four hours the

French attacked his position, enjoying a three to one numerical advantage. But once again the British refused to give ground, and for the moment Soult seemed spent. On 14 December he began to move his divisions further inland to avoid complete encirclement at Bayonne, and the British could consolidate their hold on the bloody area to the south. 'Walked over the fields,' jotted Wheatley on the 16th. 'Full of dead. Saw horrible sights. Horrid trade.'

Bayonne, with British troops positioning themselves in the sand-hills to the south of the city.

Now, on all fronts, came the lowering lull before the final, dreadful storm. Leipzig had seen the peak of Allied cooperation in the north; thereafter this cooperation rapidly declined. Austria and Prussia clashed over schemes for the future of liberated Germany; military planning suffered. Napoleon had time to recover slightly, and not until New Year's Day 1814 did the Allied armies invade eastern France, spearheaded by the Prussians under Marshal Blücher. In southern France, Wellington would have to wait even longer before a further advance: 'There are some things which *can not* be *done*,' he reported to London. 'One of them is to move troops in this country during . . . a violent fall of rain.' Storms never seemed to cease. 'Hail, snow, rain and wind, thunder and lightning,' read one of Wheatley's typical diary entries. This young lieutenant added on 27 December: 'Met Lord Wellington. He looked pale and harassed.' The Allied commander tried to ease his impatience and improve his health by hunting his foxhounds in the nearby hills, but still the storms raged over the mountains making military manoeuvre impossible. Troops occupied themselves as best they could, and found local French females by no means inhospitable – if anything more accommodating than the Spanish girls they had left behind. Nor were French troops hostile. Both sides seemed to feel that lives should be spared until battle began again: if French or British lines moved slightly forward, messages were sent politely requesting a return to the original positions; to fire on exposed sentries was usually unthinkable. Riflemen pooled their money one day and sent a man across to the French to buy brandy; the messenger unfortunately drank so much of his purchase that the French had to shout for someone to come and carry h'm back. For a few weeks war became almost civilised and even more nonsensical.

But on 25 January Napoleon quit Paris to lead his armies against the approaching Allies. And on St Valentine's Day the final push began around Bayonne. Wellington had no intention of forcing a showdown at the city; instead he detailed Sir John Hope to remain in the area while he manoeuvred Soult into open ground far to the east. For thirteen days the Allied army moved inland; Soult had to avoid being outflanked and fell back on ridges behind Orthez with 36,000 men against the Allied 31,000. Skilful manoeuvring enabled Wellington to cross the intervening rivers and by 27 February he had completed preparations for attack. By now Hope had completely besieged Bayonne. Hill received instructions to hold the enemy's attention at Orthez itself while other Allied divisions crossed the Gave de Pau river further west and struck diagonally up the spurs on to Soult's ridge. By early morning the forces had crossed the river and were pushing through the water-logged valleys to the slopes. The Bidassoa, the Nivelle, the Nive – the same pattern was now repeated. Allied troops pressed relentlessly on, the French gave ground despite fine resistance, and crumbled and fell back. 'The action was for some time very warm,' wrote Wellington to his brother, 'but I never saw troops get such a beating as they did; and they were saved at all only by night.' Wellington failed to mention the injury he had received: a spent bullet had struck his sword-hilt, driving it violently against his thigh and hip. The black bruises were especially painful when he tried to ride.

Wellington's troops were fighting superbly: polished, confident, experienced and with perfect cohesion, each part coordinating like a well-oiled machine. Yet the commander still remained unsatisfied with his veterans. 'There is no crime recorded in the Newgate Calendar that is not committed by these soldiers,' he complained from St Sever on 8 March. Wellington underlined the main problem when he added:

There is not much difficulty in posting a British army for a general action, or in getting the officers and men to do their duty in the action. The difficulty consists in bringing them to the point where the action can be fought.

And during these wet days of early spring this difficulty would have taxed any army. Wellington drove his men hard, and they responded well even if they failed to reach his required standards. Contact had been temporarily lost with the retreating French during the day after Orthez – Wellington himself had been laid on his back through his battle injury – but the army pressed on across the quagmires and rutted roads during miserable March, hoping to pin Soult against the Pyrenees. Wellington had to be carried by coach for some of the way, and normally four mules would have sufficed for pulling the vehicles, but so bad were the roads that an additional four large horses and two oxen were required, yet still the wheels became bogged to the axles in clammy clay. And these were the conditions through which the troops had to trudge, day after dismal day. Wheatley's experience seemed typical: not until 14 April would he be able to record: 'I undressed for the first time in seven weeks.' For the brave and elusive French, affairs were infinitely worse; they had one hope: Suchet, now in north-east Spain, might be able to thrust upwards to combine with Soult's forces near Toulouse on the Garonne. Toulouse therefore became the target.

And by 8 April the Garonne river had been crossed by Allied troops east and west of the city, with only Hill's forces kept south of the river opposite the suburbs. The remainder of the army began to stretch northwards between the Garonne and Ers rivers; Wellington spent most of the day reconnoitring the area. Soult had tried desperately to defend the city and the Calvinet ridge to the north, but Wellington judged these latter heights to be assailable despite the cramped area of manoeuvre caused by the nearby Ers. 197

Throughout 9 April the army moved into position; attack began at
about 6.30 am on the 10th.

    Hill's troops attempted to divert enemy attention to the south by
skirmishing and artillery fire against the St Cyprien suburbs; Soult

The Battle of Toulouse, with the allies closing in and Beresford's units advancing from the right.

remained undeceived and transferred more troops northwards to the Calvinet ridge. To the east the French commander mainly relied upon the obstacle provided by a canal which looped from the Garonne around the city outskirts. Picton's 3rd division

199

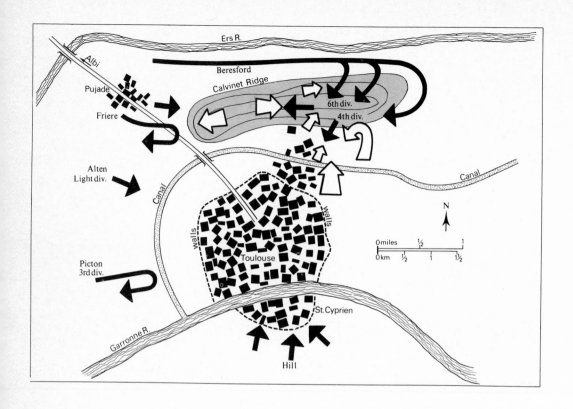

The following labels appear on the map:

Ers R.

Albi

Beresford

Calvinet Ridge

Pujade

6th div.

Friere

4th div.

Canal

Alten
Light div.

Canal

walls

N

walls

0 miles    ½    1
0 km    ½    1    1½

Picton
3rd div.

Toulouse

Garronne R.

St.Cyprien

Hill

Map 7
The Battle of Toulouse,
April 1814.

attempted a bridgehead over the water, only to be thrown back again. But Wellington's main attack was to be undertaken by Beresford's 4th and 6th divisions and by Freire's Spanish and Portuguese troops in the far north. These Allied thrusts would be aimed at the Calvinet, and entailed a long flanking march by Beresford by the bank of the Ers, while Freire struck simultaneously just to the south from Pujade village. But Beresford's advance became bogged in the cloying clay; his artillery churned the roads into sheets of grey slime. By the time Freire reached his starting position Beresford had still a muddy mile to cover – yet Freire threw his forces forward, unsupported, leading the advance himself. Within seconds these Spanish troops suffered tremendous salvoes of screeching, whistling, crashing artillery fire from the Calvinet and from the thick Toulouse walls. The air became black with tossing mud; men were thrown up screaming and mangled – and Wellington, watching through his telescope, swore, and knew the Spanish assault to be doomed. An aide galloped north with urgent orders for Beresford: the 4th and 6th divisions must strike south from their march, even though they had still to reach their

200

planned positions. But the aide had too far to travel through the squelching fields and Freire's men had now come into musket range from the rise in front, and, because of the slopes, French artillery could continue to fire over the heads of the infantry lined below. Musket and grape-shot, 'the devil's own brooms', decimated the Spanish ranks even though the brave attackers tottered on. They reached a sodden sunken road, clambered up the far bank, and tried to form line for the last forty yards to the French, but had to drop back into the ditch. And now two heavy guns from the city walls sent grape-shot splattering down the length of this road, while French troops ran from their positions to fire down upon the struggling mass of Spaniards. Survivors fled from the ditch, back over the oozing craters.

Freire's fight finished before Beresford received his order to swing south in support. Too late to give assistance, he continued along his original march for another 880 yards, then deployed the 4th and 6th divisions into line, over a front extending a mile and a half. Bugles and drums sounded the advance and the massed troops moved forward like a solid field of wind-waving scarlet poppies.

They reached the first gentle slopes and began to climb, brushing aside French skirmishers. They reached the crest on the eastern end of the ridge; two French brigades charged along the summit but failed to dislodge them. French cavalry thundered towards the left flank but met British dragoons in a clashing, sabre-ringing mêlée: arms and heads were severed by single sabre strokes, sometimes heads were sliced horizontally above the eyes, and one man rode helplessly on from the fighting with outspread arms – he had received a diagonal slash across his face which had gashed his mouth open so that his jaw hung gaping down over his crimson chest. Beresford turned the 4th division to face south towards the canal on the far side of the ridge, and deployed the 6th across the crest ready to clear the remainder of the hill. By 4 pm, after a pause to allow his field guns to move up in support, his twin advances began. Both succeeded; at the same time Freire had rallied his Spanish survivors and had struck again at the western sector of the ridge.

Night fast approached. The French pulled back over the canal in the north, except for a small bridgehead facing the 4th division. But as darkness ended the day's battle, Wellington knew his own position to be far from secure: Soult would probably attempt to re-take Calvinet ridge next day, and Beresford's men were exhausted. Yet the area remained quiet on the 11th: Soult had still to summon sufficient strength, and Wellington needed to consolidate his positions; no further attack on Toulouse could be made, although British cavalry swept south along the Ers to block French escape roads. Dwindling daylight prevented them reaching the Toulouse–Carcassonne route – and this was the road used by Soult during the night. The French had abandoned Toulouse.

Yet the battle had been needlessly fought. The war had ended even before the Toulouse struggle began, unknown to the participants. Now, as British and French clearing parties carted the unnecessary casualties from the battered battlefield – 4,568 for the Allies, 3,236 for the French – and surgeons set about their bloody work, confirmation arrived of the event which Wellington and the world had long desired. News was brought by British and French staff officers travelling together; Wellington sent them both on to Soult. Napoleon Bonaparte had abdicated almost a week ago; the capitulation of Paris had been signed at 2 am on 31 March. French tricolours were being hauled down from buildings and flag-poles throughout Europe. The Bourbon monarchy would be restored. 'You don't say so! 'Pon my honour!' exclaimed Wellington. 'Hurrah!' And he allowed himself a small jig of joy, clicking

Collar of honour presented to Wellington by King George, designed for the Peninsula campaign, but enlarged to include Waterloo.

his fingers. While Viscount Wellington of Talavera, Baron Douro, rode into Toulouse with his triumphant troops on 12 April 1814, a waxen-faced ex-Emperor writhed on his crumpled bed at Fontainebleau, his body freezing cold then burning hot, his limbs rigid, his back arched in convulsive pain, his hand over his mouth to stop vomiting out the poison he had swallowed. But Napoleon would recover in ample time for Wellington's *coup de grâce* in the fields by an unknown village named Waterloo.

Legacy of war: Chelsea Pensioners, formerly in cavalry and infantry service. The Peninsula fighting left more men maimed than even the dreadful Crimean War nearly 50 years later.

# Select Bibliography

(Anon) *Memoirs of a Sergeant, Late in the 43rd Light Infantry Regiment*, London, 1839

Bell, Douglas: *Wellington's Officers*, London, 1938

Brett-James, A. (Ed): *Wellington at War, 1794-1815*, London, 1961

'Chelsea Pensioner': *Jottings from my Sabretasch*, London, 1847

Glover, Michael: *Wellington as Military Commander, London, 1968*

Glover, Michael: *Wellington's Peninsular Victories*, London, 1963

Guedalla, Philip: *The Duke*, London, 1931

Harris: *Recollections of Rifleman Harris*, London, 1829

Hibbert, C.: *Corunna*, London, 1961

Hibbert, C. (Ed): *The Wheatley Diary*, London, 1964

Kincaid, Captain J.: *Adventures in the Rifle Brigade*, London, 1830

Longford, E.: *Wellington. The Years of the Sword*, London, 1969

Maurice, General Sir T. F. (Ed): *Diary of Sir John Moore*, London, 1904

Napier, Lieut-General William: *The Life and Opinions of General Sir Charles Napier*, 4 vols., London, 1857

Napier, Sir William F. P.: *History of the War in the Peninsula and the South of France 1807–1814* 6 vols., London, Cavendish edition, 1886

Oman, Carola: *Sir John Moore*, London, 1953

Oman, Sir C.: *A History of the Peninsular War* 7 vols., Oxford, 1902–30

Robinson, H. B.: *Memoirs of Lieut-General Sir Thomas Picton*, London, 1836

Rousseau, I. J. (Ed): *The Peninsular Journal of Major-General Sir Benjamin D'Urban*, London, 1930

Schaumann, August: *On the Road with Wellington. The Diary of a War Commissary*, London, 1924

Weller, Jac: *Wellington in the Peninsula, 1808–14*, London, 1962

Wellington (compiled by Lieut-Colonel Gurwood): *The Dispatches of Field Marshal the Duke of Wellington*, 12 vols., London, 1834–38

Wheeler, (ed Liddell-Hart): *The Letters of Private Wheeler, 1809–28*, London, 1951

# Index